A
LABOR
OF LOVE

A LABOR OF LOVE
Puritan Pastoral Priorities

J. STEPHEN YUILLE

Reformation Heritage Books
Grand Rapids, Michigan

A Labor of Love
© 2013 by J. Stephen Yuille

All rights reserved. No part of this book may be used or reproduced in any manner whatsoever without written permission except in the case of brief quotations embodied in critical articles and reviews. Direct your requests to the publisher at the following address:

Reformation Heritage Books
2965 Leonard St. NE
Grand Rapids, MI 49525
616-977-0889 / Fax 616-285-3246
orders@heritagebooks.org
www.heritagebooks.org

Printed in the United States of America
13 14 15 16 17 18/10 9 8 7 6 5 4 3 2 1

Library of Congress Cataloging-in-Publication Data

Yuille, J. Stephen, 1968-
 A labor of love : Puritan pastoral priorities / J. Stephen Yuille.
   pages cm
 Includes bibliographical references.
 ISBN 978-1-60178-266-3 (pbk. : alk. paper) 1. Pastoral theology—Puritans.
2. Pastoral theology—Reformed Church. 3. Swinnock, George, 1627-1673.
4. Pastoral theology—Biblical teaching. I. Title.
 BV4011.3.Y85 2013
 253—dc23
                        2013018131

For additional Reformed literature, request a free book list from Reformation Heritage Books at the above regular or e-mail address.

FOR THOSE ELDERS
*under whose watch I once grew
and with whose support I now serve*

Contents

Foreword. ix
Introduction.   1

PART 1

1. A Royal Ambassador.   7
2. A True Vessel. 12
3. A Sincere Suitor. 17
4. A Wise Builder 22
5. A Skilled Physician. 27
6. A Diligent Student 32
7. A Tender Mother. 37
8. A Courageous Soldier. 43
9. A Prudent Preacher. 48
10. A Ceaseless Intercessor. 55
11. A Patient Instructor. 61
12. A Discerning Judge. 67
13. A Faithful Shepherd 72
14. A Powerful Example. 77
15. A Humble Instrument 82
16. A Watchful Overseer. 87

PART 2

The Pastor's Farewell. 93
Afterword. 131
Bibliography. 135

Foreword

Many are the roles required of a pastor, his duties so numerous that in himself no man is sufficient to fulfill such a high and holy calling. It is only by the enabling grace of God that any minister of the gospel can fulfill the sacred charge laid at his feet. One way that such servants of the Lord are equipped in meeting their shepherding duties is by studying the worthy examples and trusted writings of other faithful pastors, those godly men who have so nobly gone before us.

Perhaps the greatest example of such pastoral fidelity from church history is witnessed in the Puritan divines of the sixteenth and seventeenth centuries. These were devout men, mighty in the Scripture, sound in the faith, grounded in Christ, and devoted to their flocks. The sheep entrusted to their care were constantly on their minds and ever upon their hearts. To this day, the Puritans of old remain enduring models of pastoral devotion, worthy of our careful consideration and personal emulation.

One noted Puritan example was George Swinnock (c. 1627–1673), a faithful pastor, educated at Oxford and Cambridge and made subject to the Great Ejection of 1662. So devoted was Swinnock to the full breadth of pastoral ministry that his major literary work, *The Christian Man's Calling*, contains a section on the sacred calling of a minister. In this portion, he gives sixteen prayers for every pastor to follow in their ministry.

J. Stephen Yuille has done the church a great service by extracting these prayers and placing them under sixteen headings that succinctly describe a unique facet of pastoral labor. Moreover, Yuille has enlarged upon the central truth contained within each prayer, supporting them with other Puritan quotations and his own development of thought.

Rare it is to find a book that pulls together the pastoral wisdom of a Puritan divine like Swinnock and distills it down into manageable units that are easily digestible. But this is precisely what Yuille has done in this volume. He has surveyed one of the best from the golden age of the Puritans, Swinnock, and has extracted the core teaching from this classic writing on pastoral duty. To learn from this divine is to be well-taught in ministerial responsibilities.

By reading this work and implementing it in your life, I believe that you will be better equipped in your service for Jesus Christ. May He bless you as you do His work, His way, for His glory.

Steven J. Lawson
Senior Pastor
Christ Fellowship Baptist Church
Mobile, Alabama

Introduction

Why have I written this book? That's a good question. There are a host of reasons, but two in particular merit mentioning at the outset.

First, I've written this book out of concern for *the church's diminished appreciation of pastoral ministry*. I realize this assessment might come as a surprise to some, but I'm convinced that even a casual glance at today's evangelicalism supports it. The fact that pastors act on Christ's behalf seems to rest weightless upon the church, including many pastors. What could be more important than shepherding the ones Christ purchased with His blood? What could be more crucial than watching over Christ's bride? What could be more essential than caring for Christ's body? Contrary to much of what we see and hear, pastoral ministry isn't a career choice. It's a high and holy calling.[1] "The church," writes John Stott, "lies at the very center of the eternal purpose of God."[2] It's the instrument by which God glorifies Himself in this world. That makes pastoral ministry of utmost importance.

Second, I've written this book out of concern for *the church's clouded perception of pastoral ministry*. This condition has arisen—at least in part—from our failure to differentiate between success and excellence. In simple terms, success is based upon status: an elevation of our importance in society's eyes. How does our society gauge success? It looks at things such as power, prestige, privilege,

---

1. For more on this, see John Piper, *Brothers, We Are Not Professionals: A Plea to Pastors for Radical Ministry* (Nashville: Broadman & Holman, 2002).
2. John Stott, *The Living Church* (Downers Grove, Ill.: InterVarsity, 2007), 19.

and prosperity. That view of success is ultimately rooted in pride. Sadly, today's church seems incapable (or perhaps unwilling) to acknowledge this tendency in its midst, and many insist on adopting the world's standards of success, thereby skewing notions of—among other things—the nature of pastoral ministry.

What we must grasp is that excellence stands in marked contrast to success because it isn't determined by status, but by faithfulness. In a word, it's based on an unwavering resolve to please God—no one else. As such, it's rooted in humility. Now, here's the thing that's incomprehensible (even scandalous) to large segments of today's church: *excellence is often unsuccessful*. The church needs to recapture a sense of that reality. It must recapture a sense of what's truly excellent in God's sight.

Among his last recorded words, the apostle Paul summarizes his ministry as follows: "For I am now ready to be offered, and the time of my departure is at hand. I have fought a good fight, I have finished my course, I have kept the faith: henceforth there is laid up for me a crown of righteousness, which the Lord, the righteous judge, shall give me at that day: and not to me only but unto all them that love his appearing" (2 Tim. 4:6–8). It's difficult to read these verses without my eyes clouding with tears. Paul sits in a prison cell in Rome. His eyesight is failing, and his mobility is declining. He's probably in his early sixties, but likely aged well beyond his years as a result of the multiple beatings, imprisonments, shipwrecks, and other hardships he has suffered during thirty years of ministry. As Alexander Whyte so movingly writes, Paul is "forsaken, lonely, cold and without his cloak, chained to a soldier, waiting on one of Nero's mad fits for his martyrdom."[3]

As Paul waits, what does he say? To begin with, he talks about the present—*a death worth dying* (v. 6). He describes himself as "ready to be offered." What does he mean? At this point, the *English Standard Version* is helpful. It translates Paul's words as follows:

---

3. Alexander Whyte, *Bible Characters: The New Testament* (London: Oliphants, 1952), 282.

"For I am already being poured out as a drink offering." For the context, we turn to Numbers 15, where we learn that the priests in Old Testament times poured the drink offering over the burnt offering in order to complete the sacrifice. Paul's point is that he has lived his life as a burnt offering to God. Now, it's time for the drink offering to be poured out—it's time for him to die.

Secondly, Paul talks about his past—*a life worth living* (v. 7). He provides a threefold description of his ministry: he fought the fight, he finished the course (or race), and he kept the faith. In other words, as he surveys thirty or so years of ministry, he's confident that he has been faithful. He has pursued excellence. Above all else, he has labored to glorify God.

Thirdly, Paul talks about his future—*a crown worth receiving* (v. 8). He's able to embrace martyrdom, for he knows that Christ awaits him. He's confident he will receive "a crown of righteousness." He fully expects to hear his Master say, "Well done, thou good and faithful servant" (Matt. 25:21).

My desire is to see a generation of *Pauline* pastors—men with a clear sense of their calling, coupled with an insatiable desire to please God. In other words, my desire is to see a generation of pastors committed to the pursuit of excellence. With that end in view, what can you expect in the pages that follow? The book is divided into two parts.

Part 1 consists of a series of pastoral priorities. I discovered these close to ten years ago, tucked away in a largely forgotten book: *The Christian Man's Calling*. The author is George Swinnock—a seventeenth-century English Puritan and Nonconformist (meaning he was ejected from the Church of England in 1662). In his book, Swinnock includes a small section titled "A good wish about the calling of a minister, wherein the several properties and duties of a conscientious pastor are epitomized."[4] Here he articulates his heartfelt desire for his own pastoral ministry by way of sixteen "wishes"

---

4. George Swinnock, *The Christian Man's Calling*, in *The Works of George Swinnock* (1868; repr., Edinburgh: Banner of Truth, 1992), 1:319–29.

(i.e., prayer requests). In each chapter, I include one of Swinnock's wishes (edited for the modern reader), and then expand on it with a few thoughts of my own.

Part 2 consists of a sermon (also edited for the modern reader) by George Swinnock: "The Pastor's Farewell."[5] He preached it upon his departure from St. Mary's chapel in Rickmansworth, Hertfordshire, where he had served as pastor for eleven years. In the dedication, he remarks, "There are two things which I have always judged chiefly requisite in a pastor—labor and love. The former is a work of the head, the latter a work of the heart: faithful labor will speak his love, and sincere love will sweeten his labor...both together—as soul and body are the essential parts of a man—are the whole of a minister." In this sermon, Swinnock's love for his church serves as an encouraging example for all pastors who desire to love their people in Christ.

Swinnock's insights have proven to be an invaluable guide to me over the years. My prayer is that the Lord will bless them to you—for the equipping of His ministers, the strengthening of His church, the coming of His kingdom, and the honoring of His name.

---

5. George Swinnock, "The Pastor's Farewell," in *The Works of George Swinnock* (1868; repr., Edinburgh: Banner of Truth, 1992), 4:53–100.

PART 1

ONE

A Royal Ambassador

The ministry of the Word is a calling above all others of greatest weight. The ever-blessed God has established it as the means by which He receives the deserved praise of His unique, eternal, and infinitely wise purpose, and as the means by which the Lord Jesus Christ receives the precious fruit of His bloody passion. This is accomplished by turning sinners from darkness to light and from Satan to God. In the ministry, God is pleased to commit to men—duly qualified and rightly called—the Word of reconciliation. He commands them in His name, as His ambassadors, to offer terms of peace, and to persuade and implore rebellious sinners with all earnestness and faithfulness (unless they want the blood of their people's souls required at their hands) to embrace the offer of grace and pardon. Since my God has counted me faithful, placed me in the ministry, and entrusted me with what so closely relates to His own glory, and so highly concerns the eternal happiness of precious souls, I wish in general that I might take heed to myself, and to all the flock over which the Holy Spirit has made me an overseer—to feed the church of God, which He has purchased with His own blood (Acts 20:28).

For Swinnock, pastoral ministry is "a calling above all others of greatest weight." Why? It's God's appointed means for spreading His glory and saving His people. As pastors, do we share Swinnock's conviction? God has appointed us "as His ambassadors,"

and entrusted us with "the Word of reconciliation." He has called us—as Swinnock expresses it—"to persuade and implore rebellious sinners" to accept Christ's "terms of peace." In John 7:37–38, Christ declares, "If any man thirst, let him come unto me, and drink. He that believeth on me, as the scripture hath said, out of his belly shall flow rivers of living water." In this declaration, we encounter three "terms of peace"—need, invitation, and promise.

First, Christ identifies a *need*: "If any man thirst." Here, Christ uses the imagery of physical thirst to describe a spiritual longing— what A. W. Tozer calls an "unceasing restlessness."[1] The cause of this longing is our alienation from God, which Christ describes elsewhere as "darkness" (John 8:12). The assertion that we're in "darkness" is a difficult notion for many people to accept because their worldview rests on the assumption that humanity is enlightened. They think we're progressing. Why? For starters, we can communicate with one another using cell phones and BlackBerry devices and access an incalculable amount of information via the Internet. We can travel halfway around the world in a matter of a few hours and transplant hearts and kidneys. We can build bridges that traverse the water below and towers that reach the clouds above and send spacecraft into the far reaches of the galaxy to take pictures. We can harness the power of water and wind and the energy of an atom. Based on these technological advancements, many people assume we're enlightened.

In reality, however, these things are what David Wells calls "the illusions of progress."[2] They give the impression we're moving forward, when—in actual fact—we're still in the dark. Our darkness is spiritual, in that our lives are alienated from God. Our darkness is intellectual, in that our minds are inclined to error instead of truth. Our darkness is moral, in that our hearts are inclined to evil instead of good. Despite the staggering number of changes around

---

1. A. W. Tozer, *The Pursuit of God* (Radford, Va.: Wilder, 2008), 26.
2. David F. Wells, *No Place for Truth; or, Whatever Happened to Evangelical Theology?* (Grand Rapids: Eerdmans, 1993), 59.

us, our condition remains as it has been since Adam's fall. When we perceive this darkness, the Holy Spirit creates in us a spiritual longing—the "thirst" of which Christ speaks.

Second, Christ extends an *invitation*: "Let him come unto me, and drink." Christ utters these words in the city of Jerusalem, during the Feast of Tabernacles. As part of the celebration, a priest carried a golden pitcher to the pool of Siloam, where he filled it with water, and then returned to the temple, where he poured the water into a funnel on the west side of the altar. This ritual pointed to what happened at Meribah, when the Israelites grumbled on account of their thirst. On that occasion, God declared to Moses: "Behold, I will stand before thee there upon the rock in Horeb; and thou shalt smite the rock, and there shall come water out of it, that the people may drink" (Ex. 17:6). In obedience, Moses took his rod—the rod of judgment by which God inflicted the plagues upon Egypt—and struck the rock. God stood on the rock, thereby identifying with it. Symbolically, therefore, God bore the judgment, and subsequently, the water flowed from the rock (Deut. 32:4, 15, 18, 31; Pss. 78:35; 95:1). That's the historical context for Christ's invitation. When He invites those who are thirsty to come to Him, He's claiming to be the true rock—the one who bears the rod of God's judgment.

When Adam and Eve disobeyed in the garden, they—along with all their posterity—fell into bondage to sin and death. By consequence, they fell under Satan's dominion. At that time, God ordained Satan to be the executioner of the sentence of death. Humanity's obligation to death is what gives Satan all his power. Clearly, therefore, the removal of that obligation is the termination of Satan's power. And that's precisely what Christ accomplished at the cross. In His death, He bore God's judgment in our place. In so doing, He destroyed Satan's power. John Flavel describes Christ's sacrifice as follows:

> Lord, the condemnation was Thine, that the justification might be mine. The agony was Thine, that the victory might be mine. The pain was Thine, and the ease mine. The stripes were Thine, and healing balm issuing from them mine. The vinegar and

gall were Thine, that the honey and sweet might be mine. The curse was Thine, that the blessing might be mine. The crown of thorns was Thine, that the crown of glory might be mine. The death was Thine, but the life purchased by it mine. Thou hast paid the price that I might enjoy the inheritance.[3]

We enter into the blessings of Christ's substitutionary sacrifice when we "drink" Him (i.e., believe in Him). When we eat food and drink water, we assimilate it, meaning it becomes part of our bodies. Likewise, when we eat and drink Christ, we assimilate Him. "Now we know that food," writes William Perkins, "unless it is received, will not nourish the body. Even so, unless we receive and apply Christ unto ourselves by the hand of faith, all our knowledge and assent will be as food uneaten and undigested."[4] That is to say, faith moves beyond mere intellectual assent to appropriation in the heart.

Years ago, my family and I visited Carrick-a-Rede on the coast of Northern Ireland. There's a rope-bridge, linking the mainland to a tiny island. The bridge spans 70 feet and is almost 100 feet above the sea and rocks below. Thousands of people cross the bridge every month. As I stood at the edge of that bridge, I gave mental assent to the fact that it could support my weight. However, I couldn't claim to believe it until I actually walked across it. Similarly, saving faith involves much more than mere mental assent to the gospel. According to Flavel, it involves, firstly, the understanding of the mind in regards to the truth of Christ as revealed in Scripture; secondly, the appropriation of the heart in regards to Christ as the complete remedy for sin; and, thirdly, the choice of the will in receiving Christ.[5] In other words, faith involves the entire soul. And that's how we heed Christ's invitation to drink.

---

3. John Flavel, *The Fountain of Life: A Display of Christ in His Essential and Mediatorial Glory*, in *The Works of John Flavel* (1820; repr., London: Banner of Truth, 1968), 1:101.

4. William Perkins, *A Godly and Learned Exposition upon Christ's Sermon on the Mount*, in *The Works of William Perkins* (London: John Legate, 1631), 3:245.

5. Flavel, *Fountain of Life*, 2:129–34.

Third, Christ issues a *promise*: "He that believeth on me, as the scripture hath said, out of his belly shall flow rivers of living water." According to the next verse, the "living water" is the Holy Spirit. Once the rock (Christ) is struck, the water (Holy Spirit) flows. When we believe in Christ, we become partakers of the Holy Spirit who brings us into fellowship with God. We rest in Him as the dearest Father, wisest guide, strongest shield, greatest good, closest friend, kindest comfort, finest beauty, deepest truth, and sweetest love. As a result, our longing is satisfied; our thirst is quenched. In a word, we're "filled with all the fullness of God" (Eph. 3:19).

As pastors, we proclaim these "terms of peace." We proclaim the gospel—the good news that God saves sinners from His wrath for His glory through Christ's substitutionary death. And this message makes "the ministry of the Word…a calling above all others of greatest weight."

TWO

A True Vessel

I wish that I might know experimentally what regeneration means, before I preach to others. I wish that I might dissuade them from sin, and persuade them to receive the Savior, out of my knowledge of the bitterness of the first and the sweetness of the second. Let me not—like some chefs—prepare food, which I do not eat, for others. May my sermons be the travail of my soul—that I might serve my God with my spirit in the gospel of His Son. As a true vessel of the sanctuary, may I have within me a savor of the water of life, which I pour out for others. It is terrible to fall into hell from the pew. But how dreadful it is to fall into hell from the pulpit! Does not my heart tremble to think that it is possible for me—like the unbelieving spies—to survey the heavenly Canaan, yet never possess it (Num. 14:36–38)? Does not my heart tremble to think that, while I preach to others, I might be a castaway? Lord, let me so exalt Thee in my heart as my chief good, in my life as my utmost end, and preach so effectually to myself and others, that I might both save myself and those who hear me (1 Tim. 4:16).

As a young boy, I really enjoyed my town's fall fair with its bounty of rides and exhibits. One of my favorites was the house of mirrors. Some of the mirrors exaggerated height, while others exaggerated width. All of them reflected a distorted image. The sad reality is that many people live in what's akin to a house of mirrors. By that, I mean they live with a distorted view of themselves—not of their bodies, but of their souls. They have a skewed perspective of their condition before God.

In the above quote, Swinnock acknowledges that it's possible for even a pastor to live in a house of mirrors—that is, to deceive himself into thinking he's something he isn't. Swinnock doesn't believe he's above such self-deception, and so he prays that he "might know experimentally what regeneration means." For Swinnock, such experimental knowledge comes when God is exalted in our hearts as the "chief good" and in our lives as the "utmost end." What does he mean? The place to begin is with his definition of regeneration. He describes it as "a work of God's Spirit, whereby He does, out of His mere good pleasure, for His own glory and the salvation of His elect, at first renew the whole man after His own image by the ministry of the Word."[1] To state it simply, Swinnock believes regeneration is the renewal of God's image in us.

The fact that God must renew His image in us implies that it has been lost. In *The Holy War,* John Bunyan uses powerful imagery to depict this loss:

> When the giant had thus engarrisoned himself in the town of Mansoul...he set himself to defacing. Now there was in the marketplace in Mansoul, and also upon the gates of the castle, an image of the blessed King Shaddai. This image was so exactly engraved...that it did the most resemble Shaddai of anything that was then present in the world. This he basely commanded to be defaced, and it was as basely done by the hand of Mr. No-Truth.... He likewise gave order that the same Mr. No-Truth should set up in its stead the horrid and formidable image of Diabolus, to the great contempt of the former King, and debasing of his town of Mansoul.[2]

---

1. George Swinnock, *The Door of Salvation Opened by the Key of Regeneration,* in *The Works of George Swinnock* (1868; repr., Edinburgh: Banner of Truth, 1992), 1:319–29.

2. John Bunyan, *The Holy War: The Losing and Taking Again of the Town of Mansoul* (Grand Rapids: Baker, 1991), 23.

When the giant assails Mansoul, he immediately defaces the image of Shaddai, replacing it with the image of Diabolus. Bunyan's point is that, at the time of Adam's fall, humanity lost the image of God. The faculties of the soul (understanding, affections, and will) characterized by knowledge, righteousness, and holiness constitute the image of God in humanity (Eph. 4:24; Col. 3:10).

When Adam sinned, the image of God was corrupted. That doesn't mean Adam lost his faculties; on the contrary, his soul still consisted of understanding, affections, and will. Rather, it means he lost knowledge, righteousness, and holiness, and this deprivation had a negative impact upon Adam's faculties. His will was no longer directed by an understanding that knew God or affections that desired God. Rather, his understanding was darkened, his affections were hardened, and his will was enslaved. This has been the predicament of his posterity ever since.

For Swinnock, regeneration is the renewal of God's image, meaning the faculties of the soul are renewed in knowledge, righteousness, and holiness. At the time of regeneration, the Holy Spirit illuminates the darkened understanding, softens the hardened affections, and liberates the enslaved will. As a result of this renewal, we possess a new spiritual sense. We take God as our "chief good" and "utmost end." Swinnock declares, "According to the excellency of the object which we embrace in our hearts, such is the degree of our happiness; the saint's choice is right, God alone being the soul's center and rest."[3]

In a word, we embrace God as incomparable. His incomparable power draws forth faith from our hearts. His incomparable wisdom draws forth fear from our hearts. His incomparable goodness draws forth love from our hearts. These three *graces* cause our hearts to close with God as our center and rest. That is to say, we take God as our happiness; we take God's Son as our Savior; we take God's Spirit

---

3. George Swinnock, *The Fading of the Flesh and the Flourishing of Faith*, in *The Works of George Swinnock* (1868; repr., Edinburgh: Banner of Truth, 1992), 4:2.

as our guide; we take God's Word as our rule; we take God's holiness as our desire; and we take God's promises as our hope. Jonathan Edwards is on the mark when he writes, "Such a difference is there between true saints and natural men: natural men have no sense of the…excellency of holy things…. But the saints, by the mighty power of God, have it discovered to them. They have that supernatural, most noble and divine sense given them, by which they perceive it; and it is this that captivates their hearts, and delights them above all things."[4]

As pastors, what "captivates" our hearts? What "delights" us above all else? For over thirty years, I lived within a two-hour drive of Niagara Falls. Apparently, more than twelve million tourists visit Niagara Falls each year. To be honest, I don't know what all the fuss is about. Why is that? Proximity and familiarity have dulled my sense of amazement. Sadly, the same thing can happen to our appreciation of the things of God. We've read that verse so many times that it no longer moves us. We've sung that hymn so many times that it no longer grips us. We've participated at the Lord's Supper so many times that it no longer stirs us. We've heard about our sin so many times that it no longer breaks our hearts. We've heard about Christ's atonement so many times that it no longer warms our hearts. We've heard about God's mercy so many times that it no longer melts our hearts. Proximity and familiarity can dull our sense of amazement.

A dwindling appreciation of the things of God is hazardous because we crave the *experience* of amazement. And the devil tempts us to seek it in all the wrong places. Some of us seek it in a new cause or new house or new relationship. Some of us seek it in materialism—the latest fashion or gadget. Some of us seek it in virtual reality. These things provide a temporary buzz. Ultimately, however, they leave us empty. As pastors, we are far from immune to this danger. Therefore, we must strive to keep our hearts fixed on God. The heart is like a violin—if abused or neglected, it loses its

---

4. Jonathan Edwards, *Religious Affections* (Minneapolis: Bethany House, 1996), 103.

tuning. As a violin requires a musician to keep it in tune, our hearts require constant communion with God to keep them in tune. This is Swinnock's desire. He wants God to be so exalted in his heart that he might be a "true vessel," possessing within him a "savor of the water of life," which he can pour out for others.

THREE

A Sincere Suitor

I wish that the spring of my actions, and the principle of my work, might be love for my Master and not the expectation of temporal reward. Oh, that I might never be so sinful as to sell the incomparable Savior for a little corruptible silver, or to turn my Father's house into a house of merchandise. May my sincere affection for the bleeding Head, and tender compassion for His blessed members, be all the oil needed to feed the lamp by which I enlighten others in the way to life. Oh, may the affectionate exhortation of my dear Redeemer echo in my ears, and pierce my soul, "Feed my lambs.... Feed my sheep" (John 21:15, 17). I desire that my purpose in ministry might be to exalt the glorious name of my God in the conversion and edification of His precious and chosen ones. I desire that I might not use preaching—as a thief uses a picklock—to open people's wallets, but as a key to open their hearts, so that the truth of God, and the God of truth, might enter. Why should I profane so pious an ordinance by pretending to serve my Savior? Let me not, like Balaam, minister for money (Num. 22–24). Let me not, through covetousness, turn inestimable souls into mere merchandise. Christ considered them to be worth His precious blood. Oh, that I might not seek my people's goods, but their good; not my profit, but their profit. Lord, let this design lie at the bottom of my heart in every act of my office. May I be like Abraham's steward, who provided a wife for his master's son (Gen. 24:2–4). Enable me to set forth the beauty of His person, the excellence of His precepts, and the vastness of His portion, so that I might woo to purpose, and present my people as a chaste virgin to Christ.

What is the "spring" of our actions—the "principle" of our work? That's a challenging question. Swinnock raises the issue because he recognizes the peril of engaging in pastoral ministry for the wrong motive. He identifies the "expectation of temporal reward" as particularly threatening. Temporal reward takes many forms, with glory as one of the most common. As pastors, self-love is a constant hazard that will entice us to use the ministry (and people) as a means of self-promotion. When facing this temptation, we must remember Paul's conviction: "So then neither is he that planteth any thing, neither he that watereth; but God that giveth the increase" (1 Cor. 3:7).

If Paul were alive today, he wouldn't seek glory for himself. He wouldn't desire to make a name for himself. He wouldn't want to draw any attention to himself. He wouldn't start a church bearing his name, or a ministry bearing his name, or an organization bearing his name. He wouldn't use gimmicks. He wouldn't manufacture controversy in order to get attention. He wouldn't be verbally edgy or culturally savvy or create a cult of personality. And he wouldn't turn the Christian faith into a means by which he could stroke his overinflated ego.

Another form of temporal reward is money. Again turning to Paul, we hear him reminding the Thessalonian believers: "For neither at any time used we flattering words, as ye know, nor a cloak of covetousness; God is witness" (1 Thess. 2:5). If Paul were alive today, he wouldn't (in Swinnock's words) "use preaching—as a thief uses a picklock—to open people's wallets." Paul wouldn't drive a Bentley or appear on stage with coiffed hair and expensive suits. He wouldn't market the gospel—or himself. He wouldn't plaster his face on billboards. He wouldn't say that God willed his financial prosperity or define the abundant life in terms of material wealth. He definitely wouldn't turn the Christian faith into a commercial enterprise.

Do we minister for "temporal reward?" What is the "spring" of our actions—the "principle" of our work? As Swinnock makes clear, the only acceptable motive is "sincere affection for the bleeding Head, and tender compassion for His blessed members." In other words, pastoral ministry must flow out of love for God and His people; therefore, we must ensure that our love is sincere. Paul declares, "Let love be without dissimulation" (Rom. 12:9). The *English Standard Version* translates his words as follows: "Let love be genuine." The term "dissimulation" (or "genuine") is *anupokritos*—without a mask.

In Greek drama productions, actors wore masks in order to depict their characters' emotions. But an actor might actually have been feeling something entirely different from the emotion displayed by his mask. The mask might have been sad when he was happy. The mask might have been happy when he was sad. Paul's point is that, when it comes to love, we must not wear masks. We must not give people the impression that we love them (kind words, warm hugs, beautiful smiles, firm handshakes), when in reality we feel quite different. We must not deceive ourselves into thinking that externals will *mask* what lurks inside. We must avoid the peril of hiding behind what Jonathan Edwards calls "excellent privileges" and "excellent performances."[1] We must make certain that there's a correlation between our hearts and our actions. In short, we must be sincere.

According to James Boice, the English word *sincere* comes from two Latin words: *sine cera* (without wax). In the ancient world, merchants would use wax to hide cracks and defaults in their pottery, so that they could sell their merchandise at higher prices.[2] But more reputable merchants would hang a sign over their pottery—*sine cera* (without wax)—to inform their customers that their merchandise was the genuine article. Our love must be sincere. It must be the principle from which we pray, preach, encourage, rebuke, exhort, and disciple. It must be the principle from which we seek to point people to Christ—or (as Swinnock puts it) to "woo to purpose."

As recorded in Genesis 24, Abraham sends his servant to the land of his forefathers to find a bride for Isaac. His servant makes

---

1. Jonathan Edwards, *Charity and Its Fruits: Christian Love as Manifested in the Heart and Life* (1852; repr., Edinburgh: Banner of Truth, 2000), 3.
2. James M. Boice, *Romans: The New Humanity* (Grand Rapids: Baker, 1995), 1591.

the journey and meets Rebekah by the well at Nahor. In his conversation with Rebekah, he says many things, including this: "I am Abraham's servant. And the LORD hath blessed my master greatly; and he is become great.... And Sarah my master's wife bare a son to my master when she was old: and unto him hath he given all that he hath" (vv. 34–36). Why does Abraham's servant say all that? What's he doing? In a word, he's wooing Rebekah. To *woo* means to entice. He mentions that Abraham is great, and that he has given everything to Isaac, because he's trying to persuade Rebekah to accept the marriage proposal.

That's a beautiful picture of the work of the Holy Spirit, who *woos* us. He persuades us to marry Christ. In effect, He says, "The Father has greatly blessed the Son, so that He has become great… and He has given all that He has to the Son." Christ confirms that very thing in John 16:15, declaring, "All things the Father hath are mine." This is our role as pastors. Out of sincere love, we proclaim Christ to our people, setting forth (in Swinnock's words) "the beauty of His person, the excellence of His precepts, and the vastness of His portion."

As pastors, we must be thoroughly convinced that there's nothing more soul-satisfying than contemplating Christ and our interest in Him. In the words of John Owen, "Unto them that believe unto the saving of the soul, [Christ] is, He always has been, precious—the sun, the rock, the life, the bread of their souls—everything that is good, useful, amiable, desirable, here or unto eternity."[3] Therefore, we must encourage our people to look continually "unto Jesus the author and finisher of our faith" (Heb. 12:2).

We must encourage them to behold Christ in His manifold roles and relations. As Redeemer, He delivers us from sin. As Mediator, He reconciles us to God. As Husband, He unites us to Himself. As Father, He cares for us. As Priest, He intercedes for us. As Shepherd,

---

3. John Owen, *A Declaration of the Glorious Mystery of the Person of Christ—God and Man*, in *The Works of John Owen*, ed. W. H. Gould (1850; repr., Edinburgh: Banner of Truth, 1977), 1:3.

He leads and protects us. As Prophet, He instructs and illuminates us. As Advocate, He pleads for us. As Friend, He loves us with fervent affection. As King, He rules over us. As Surety, He guarantees our inheritance. As Rock, He satisfies us. "Look on [Christ]," urges John Flavel, "in what respect or particular you will; cast your eye upon this lovely object, and view Him any way; turn Him in your serious thoughts which way you will; consider His person, His offices, His works, or any other thing belonging to Him; you will find Him altogether lovely."[4]

---

4. John Flavel, *The Method of Grace in the Gospel Redemption*, in *The Works of John Flavel* (1820; repr., London: Banner of Truth, 1968), 2:215. The expression "altogether lovely" is found in Song of Solomon 5:16.

FOUR

A Wise Builder

My work is great because it is for God, not man. For this reason, I wish that God might equip and enable me—like Bezaleel and Aholiab (Ex. 36:1–2)—for the building of His spiritual temple. I desire that—like a wise builder—I might lay the foundation of sound doctrine, establish the strong pillars of convincing reasons, and cover them with useful and powerful applications. May I be so thoroughly furnished unto every good work that I might upon all occasions bring out of my treasury things new and old. Lord, let a double portion of Thy Spirit be poured on me! Let Thy blessing so prosper my studies that I might be an "able minister of the new testament; not of the letter, but of the Spirit" (2 Cor. 3:6), and "a workman that needeth not to be ashamed, rightly dividing the word of truth" (2 Tim. 2:15).

Swinnock desires to be a "wise builder," laying "the foundation of sound doctrine," establishing "the strong pillars of convincing reasons," and covering them with "useful and powerful applications." His desire flows from his conviction that Scripture is God's Word. The apostle Paul declares, "All scripture is given by inspiration of God, and is profitable for doctrine, for reproof, for correction, for instruction in righteousness: that the man of God may be perfect, thoroughly furnished unto all good works" (2 Tim. 3:16–17). When we speak of Scripture, we're referring of course to the Old Testament and New Testament.

We receive the Old Testament as Scripture, because Christ *authenticated* it. How? To begin with, He received the Old Testament, recognizing as Scripture the Jewish tripartite division of the Law, the Prophets, and the Psalms (Luke 24:44–45). Moreover, He quoted the Old Testament, employing it to resist trials, construct arguments, silence critics, teach lessons, reveal prophecies, defend truths, and expose needs. Finally, He accepted the Old Testament as historical, referring to specific events (e.g., the first marriage, the flood, the destruction of Sodom, and the burning bush) and individuals (e.g., Adam, Eve, Abel, Abraham, Isaac, Jacob, Noah, Moses, David, Solomon, Elijah, Elisha, Naaman, and Jonah).

We receive the New Testament as Scripture because Christ *authorized* it. How? He declared to His disciples: "as my Father hath sent me, even so I send you" (John 20:21). That is to say, Christ invested His disciples with authority, thereby making them His authorized representatives. As such, they served as the church's foundation (Eph. 2:19–22). And in that role, they gave the New Testament to the church. As B. B. Warfield explains, "We rest our acceptance of the New Testament Scriptures...not on the fact that they are the product of the revelation-age of the church, for so are many other books which we do not thus accept; but on the fact that God's authoritative agents in founding the church gave them as authoritative to the church which they founded.... It is clear that prophetic and apostolic origin is the very essence of the authority of the Scriptures."[1]

Two texts are particularly helpful for understanding what Paul means when he asserts, "All scripture is given by inspiration of God" (or, as in the ESV, "breathed out by God"). The first is Romans 9:17, where he writes, "For the scripture saith unto Pharaoh, 'Even for this same purpose have I raised thee up....'" Here, Paul refers to Exodus 9:16. When we turn there, however, we discover that it was

---

1. B. B. Warfield, "The Authority and Inspiration of the Scriptures," in *Westminster Teacher* (September 1889), n.p., available online, http://www.theologynetwork.org/christian-beliefs/the-bible/the-authority-and-inspiration-of-the-scriptures.htm.

actually *God* who said to Pharaoh, "Even for this same purpose have I raised thee up." So, why does Paul affirm that the Scripture said it, when—in actual fact—God said it? The answer: "All scripture is given by inspiration of God."

The second text is Matthew 19:4–5, where Christ responds to the Pharisees' query concerning divorce: "Have ye not read, that he which made them at the beginning made them male and female, and said, For this cause shall a man leave father and mother, and shall cleave to his wife: and the twain shall be one flesh?" According to what Christ says here, God created the first man and woman and said that a man shall "leave father and mother" and "cleave to his wife." Yet, upon turning to Genesis 2:24, we discover that God didn't utter these words. Moses penned them. So, why does Christ affirm that God said it, when—in actual fact—Moses wrote it? The answer: "All scripture is given by inspiration of God."

When we affirm that "All scripture is given by inspiration of God," we mean that the Holy Spirit used the human authors in such a way that what they wrote was His, not theirs. The Scripture is the Word of God. For this reason, we affirm its authority and sufficiency. "Hath God said?" was Satan's question to Eve (Gen. 3:1). His intent was to create doubt in Eve's mind about the reliability of God's Word. The battle over the authority and sufficiency of God's Word has raged ever since.

Early in its history, the church confronted Gnosticism and Montanism. This struggle contributed—at least in part—to the church's recognition of the New Testament canon. At the time of the Reformation, the church again engaged in a major battle over God's Word. On one front, it resisted Roman Catholicism—the belief that the church's oral tradition is as authoritative as Scripture. On another front, it resisted Quakerism—the belief that the individual's "inner light" is as authoritative as Scripture.

The battle continues to rage in our day. At present, the church is engaged in four key conflicts. The first is with rationalism. According to this view, human reason is the measure of all truth, and natural religion must take precedence over revealed religion.

Therefore, the Christian faith must be reduced to truths that we can derive from nature.

The second conflict is with incarnationalism, which holds that the process of inspiration is like Christ's incarnation. In other words, God's Word comes clothed in human language and culture, and some of this clothing is time-bound and culturally specific. The result is a mixture of God's truth and cultural myth, meaning we must separate the two in order to arrive at the meaning of Scripture.

The third conflict is with relativism. Proponents of this view believe absolute truth is unknowable; therefore, the original intent of the biblical authors is unknowable, and so they embrace the postmodern concept of the centrality of community. Scripture is interpreted (and truth determined) within specific communities through the ongoing, illuminating work of the Holy Spirit.

The fourth conflict is with mysticism. According to this view, the Holy Spirit speaks directly to individuals. Proponents separate the Holy Spirit's ministry from the Word and unquestioningly follow their hunches, impulses, intuitions, and feelings—daring to label them God's voice.

All of these views serve to undermine the authority and sufficiency of Scripture. We reject these views, affirming Scripture alone as the Word of God.[2] Its *efficient* cause is God: the "glorious and supreme Majesty of heaven and earth." Its *moving* cause is the Holy Spirit, whereby "the penman and scribes…were men extraordinarily inspired." Its *instrumental* cause is the provision of a "perfect rule," which "informs us fully in our carriage towards God, and towards men." Its *formal* cause is the stimulation of our "highest esteem and hottest affection," because of its "exact conformity to the will of God." And its *final* cause is "the glory of the great God, and the salvation of lost man."

For Swinnock, these five causes demonstrate that Scripture is "the rule of all truth." He adds, "It is not what sense says, or reason says, or what fathers say, or what general councils say, or what

---

2. Swinnock, *Christian Man's Calling*, 2:430–34.

traditions say, or what customs say, but what Scripture says. That is to be the rule of faith and life. Whatever is contrary to Scripture, or beside Scripture, or not rationally deducible from Scripture, is to be rejected as spurious and adulterate."[3]

Scripture isn't the product of human invention. Rather, it's the Word of God. As such, it's the means by which God reveals Himself to us and imparts His grace to us. It's the instrument by which the Holy Spirit effects our union with Christ and the way Christ comes to us. For that reason, Scripture stands at the center of the life of the Christian and the church. A "wise builder" stands on this foundation.

---

3. Swinnock, *Christian Man's Calling*, 2:440.

FIVE

A Skilled Physician

Since I am a steward of the mysteries of Christ, I wish that I might be true to the souls of my people. Let me not sow pillows under men's elbows for any gain or advantage, but be a Barnabas (a son of encouragement to the penitent) and a Boanerges (a son of thunder to the presumptuous). Knowing the terror of the Lord, may I persuade people, and give to everyone their proper portion in due season. Oh, let me not be like Ahab's four hundred prophets, who sold their king's life at the cheap rate of a lie (1 Kings 22:6). Let me be like Micaiah—careful to distribute food that is suitable and wholesome to their spiritual conditions. Although my patients might become angry when I probe their infected wounds, they will thank me when they recover. If I am afraid to tell people about their sins, I murder their souls. Lord, when I am visiting my people in private, or preaching to them in public, cause me to hear Thy voice: "When I say unto the wicked, Thou shalt surely die; and thou givest him not warning, nor speakest to warn the wicked from his wicked way, to save his life; the same wicked man shall die in his iniquity; but his blood will I require at thine hand" (Ezek. 3:18).

Here, Swinnock expresses his desire to be like the prophet Micaiah. Who was Micaiah? All we know of this obscure prophet comes from an incident involving Ahab (king of Israel) and Jehoshaphat (king of Judah). These two kings plan to attack the city of Ramothgilead, which had fallen under Syrian control. Before committing himself to battle, Jehoshaphat asks Ahab to consult "the word of the LORD" (1 Kings 22:5). He wants to know if God is in favor of their plans. In response, Ahab gathers his four hundred prophets, who assure the kings of God's blessing upon their endeavor. But Jehoshaphat knows these prophets are on Ahab's payroll. And so, he asks, "Is there not here a prophet of the LORD besides, that we might inquire of him?" (v. 7). Reluctantly, Ahab sends a messenger to summon the prophet Micaiah. When the messenger finds Micaiah, he encourages him to conform to the favorable message already delivered by Ahab's four hundred prophets. But Micaiah replies, "As the LORD liveth, what the LORD saith unto me, that will I speak" (v. 14).

For Swinnock, Micaiah is an exemplar of faithfulness in the midst of faithlessness, and he longs to be like him. In the context of his ministry, Swinnock knows such faithfulness implies telling "people about their sins"—even if it means incurring their displeasure. Similarly, as pastors, we need to be convinced of our responsibility to tell people what God thinks of their sin. Like a skilled physician, we must be willing to probe their wounds.

Prior to departing for a trip to Ireland in 1999, my wife and I dutifully turned off the electricity in our apartment. However, we neglected to empty the fridge and freezer. We were living in Portugal at the time. It was July—the warmest month of the year. Two weeks later, we returned to our home, unaware of what was lurking behind the door. When I opened it, the smell of the putrefying meat was so strong that I nearly fell to my knees. That's but a glimpse of what our sin is like in God's sight. As Swinnock explains:

> Original sin has debauched the mind, and made it think crooked things straight, and straight things crooked; loathsome things lovely, and lovely things loathsome. It has perverted the will, and made it, as a diseased stomach, to eat unwholesome food against reason. It has enthralled the affections to sensuality and brutishness. It has chained the whole man, and delivered it up to the law of sin. It has bound reason and conscience in chains.[1]

---

1. Swinnock, *Christian Man's Calling*, 2:166.

Here, Swinnock affirms that original sin has "debauched" the mind, "perverted" the will, and "enthralled" the affections. In essence, original sin has "chained the whole man." Robert Bolton echoes this sentiment, stating, "My mind is blind, vain, foolish, my will perverse and rebellious, all my affections out of order, there is nothing whole or sound within me."[2]

That has been the predicament of Adam's posterity ever since the fall. Because of the corruption of his nature, Adam could not transmit the perfect nature of his soul to his descendants. Instead, he transmitted the corrupt nature acquired by the fall. As a result, all of us are "dead in trespasses and sins" (Eph. 2:1). In a word, sin has dominion over us. At times, this dominion is obvious, meaning some of us live with the visible effects and consequences of sin. It takes a toll on our bodies, families, and communities.

I lectured for several years at Toronto Baptist Seminary, located on Jarvis Street—a rough part of town. I didn't need to walk very far to see someone passed out drunk on a park bench or a prostitute on a street corner. In such cases, sin's dominion is obvious. At other times, however, sin's dominion isn't so obvious; it's secret and hidden. But it's just as real, just as powerful, and just as wicked. Sin has many manifestations, but it only has one root: self-centeredness.

Robert Louis Stevenson captures this reality in *The Strange Case of Dr. Jekyll and Mr. Hyde*. The main character, Dr. Henry Jekyll, is a respectable man who harbors secret inclinations to evil. He would like to act on them, but he's afraid of the consequences. One day, however, he invents a potion that will transform his appearance, enabling him to indulge his evil inclinations in secret. Upon drinking the potion for the first time, he becomes Mr. Edward Hyde: "I knew myself, at the first breath of this new life, to be more wicked, tenfold more wicked, sold a slave to my original evil; and the thought, in that moment, braced and delighted me like wine."[3]

---

2. Robert Bolton, *The Carnal Professor, Discovering the Woeful Slavery of a Man Guided by the Flesh* (1634; repr., Ligonier, Pa.: Soli Deo Gloria, 1992), 19.

3. Robert Louis Stevenson, *Dr. Jekyll and Mr. Hyde*, in *Robert Louis Stevenson: Four Complete Novels* (New York: Gramercy, 1995), 398–99.

As Mr. Hyde, he indulges all sorts of evil desires. When the potion wears off, he transforms back into Dr. Jekyll. And no one knows the difference. After a while, however, Dr. Jekyll's sinful indulgence begins to frighten him, and his conscience begins to disturb him. In desperation, he vows never to take the potion again. Moreover, he vows to atone for his misdeeds by committing himself to a life of good works. As time passes, Dr. Jekyll is increasingly impressed with himself: "And then I smiled, comparing myself with other men, comparing my active goodwill with the lazy cruelty of their neglect. And at the very moment of that vain-glorious thought, a qualm came over me, a horrid nausea and the most deadly shuddering…I looked down…I was once more Edward Hyde."[4]

Dr. Jekyll hadn't taken the potion. But, involuntarily, he had transformed into Mr. Hyde. Why? His good works can't *hide* what he is inside. As a matter of fact, they actually bring out what he truly is. They aggravate his self-centeredness, and foster his self-righteousness. They feed his pride. Dr. Jekyll is Mr. Hyde.

That's us. We try to hide what we are in a veneer of respectability. But there are times when what's hidden comes into view—fits of rage, lust, and envy. These moments show us who we really are. Our efforts to compensate with our works, traditions, disciplines, and regulations are useless. They merely serve to feed the root of our sin—self-centeredness. That's the essence of sin. As pastors, we must proclaim it—no matter the cost. Very few people will object to hearing they do *bad* things, but almost everyone will object to hearing they never do any *good* things. Why? The root of sin is self-centeredness, which always manifests itself in self-righteousness.

As we "tell people about their sins," we strive—as Swinnock puts it—to be like Boanerges: "a son of thunder to the presumptuous." Equally important, we strive to be like Barnabas: "a son of encouragement to the penitent." That means we never lose sight of the relationship between truth and grace. They're inseparable companions. Truth cuts, but grace heals. Truth stings, but grace soothes.

---

4. Stevenson, *Dr. Jekyll and Mr. Hyde*, 405.

Truth disturbs, but grace comforts. Truth demands that we declare what a righteous God says.

With all earnestness, we seek to convey what He thinks about sin. However, grace demands that we declare what a compassionate God says. While we declare His utter displeasure with sin and sinners, we do so against the backdrop of His abounding mercy. Where there's brokenness for sin, He promises healing. Where there's conviction of sin, He promises mercy. Where there's weariness for sin, He promises rest. Where there's repentance for sin, He promises forgiveness. Grace always proclaims what God says, from the shadow of the cross.

SIX

A Diligent Student

I desire that I might not be condemned as a wicked servant, hiding my sins in the cloak of excuses, or as a slothful servant, hiding my talent in the napkin of idleness. May I mind the work of the ministry, and make it evident that—in my preparation for and execution of my office—I labor in the Word and doctrine. My time and gifts are not my own, but under God. I must use them for my people's benefit. My prayer is that I might not offer to the Lord my God that which costs me nothing. I pray that the food, which I set before my people, may not be half-baked—unsuitable for their stomachs to digest—because of my negligence in preparing it. I pray that I might devote myself to reading Scripture, meditating on it, and giving myself to it, so that all may see my progress (1 Tim. 4:13–15). My output is considerable and, therefore, my input must be answerable. Surely, if anyone should study hard, read hard, and pray hard, it should be those who feed God's children. I wish that I might be industrious in building the temple, and cheerfully exhaust myself in Christ's service. Some people thought our Savior was fifty years old, when He was only thirty. His excessive ministry made Him to appear older. Oh, my soul, follow His blessed example! Do not play, "but work the works of him that sent [you]" (John 9:4). Use all opportunities to the utmost. Be ready in season and out of season. Serve your God with all your strength. Like fuel, consume yourself, in order to warm the saint's cold heart and thaw the sinner's frozen heart. Your work is of infinite consequence, your time is exceedingly short, and your reward is glorious and eternal. Consume yourself, in order to prevent their endless woe.

Be a fruitful mother, who bears new children, even if it costs you much pain and sorrow—perhaps even your life.

With Paul's admonition before him (1 Tim. 4:13–15), Swinnock asks God to help him as he seeks to devote himself "to reading Scripture, meditating on it, and giving [himself] to it." Why's this so important in Swinnock's eyes? He wants his "progress" (i.e., growth) to be evident to all.

As pastors, this is crucial. In the first place, we don't devote ourselves to Scripture in order to prepare sermons or write books or teach classes. We devote ourselves to Scripture in order to grow. Far too many of us are prone to feeding others while starving ourselves. Many of us fall into the error of equating our spiritual maturity with our biblical and theological knowledge.[1] While important, mere knowledge isn't an end in itself. We need to remember that there's a difference between knowing with the head (*theoretical, notional, speculative* knowledge) and knowing with the heart (*practical, inclinational, sensible* knowledge). To put it another way, there's a difference between *thinking* that honey is sweet and *tasting* that honey is sweet. Far too many pastors fail to close the gap between these two: the head and the heart. With that challenge in view, we must devote ourselves to God's Word.

When we read, we seek to avoid two potential dangers. First, we avoid the danger of a subjective reading of Scripture: we don't approach it superficially, seeking some sort of intuitive response. Second, we avoid the danger of a rationalistic reading of Scripture: we recognize that it isn't a mere textbook but God's Word addressed to His people. We avoid these two dangers because we're committed to the grammatical-historical study of Scripture. We believe we must strive to ascertain the meaning of each biblical text. But we

---

1. For a helpful treatment of this subject, see Paul Tripp, *Dangerous Calling: Confronting the Unique Challenges of Pastoral Ministry* (Wheaton, Ill.: Crossway, 2012).

also believe that, as we do the hard work of study, we must apply our minds to what Swinnock calls "sacred subjects" as they appear in God's Word. These serve as "windows," whereby "beams" enter the soul, enlightening the mind and warming the affections.[2] Swinnock gives three helpful pieces of advice for reading Scripture.

First, in terms of our "preparation," we empty our hearts of "evil frames and prejudice."[3] In other words, we rid ourselves of anything that impedes Scripture's entrance into the soul. By way of example, Swinnock appeals to the Israelites' loathing of the manna in the wilderness.[4] God provided manna in order to sustain them on their journey to the Promised Land, but they grew tired of it because they remembered what they had eaten in Egypt: the cucumbers, melons, leeks, and onions (Num. 11:5–6). As a result, they despised the manna. Swinnock's point is that we must lay aside whatever "trash" dulls our appetite for God's Word.[5] We must labor to impress upon our hearts Scripture's inestimable worth. "It is," says he, "the voice of God."[6] With this proper appreciation of Scripture in place, we entreat God to open our eyes to see, our ears to hear, and our hearts to receive.[7]

Second, in terms of our "carriage" while reading Scripture, we set ourselves seriously in the presence of God.[8] Then, we apply Scripture to our lives.[9] Whether it's the curses and commands of the law, or the comforts of the gospel, we appropriate them by faith. Moreover, we permit Scripture to come with authority to our consciences.[10] To sum up, Swinnock believes we must "eat the word."[11] In other words, we must internalize it. We believe that God is its author, that its precepts and promises are directed at us, and we read and hear it

---

2. Swinnock, *Christian Man's Calling*, 2:426.
3. Swinnock, *Christian Man's Calling*, 1:145.
4. Swinnock, *Christian Man's Calling*, 1:146.
5. Swinnock, *Christian Man's Calling*, 1:146.
6. Swinnock, *Christian Man's Calling*, 1:151.
7. Swinnock, *Christian Man's Calling*, 1:153.
8. Swinnock, *Christian Man's Calling*, 1:156.
9. Swinnock, *Christian Man's Calling*, 1:157–59.
10. Swinnock, *Christian Man's Calling*, 1:159.
11. Swinnock, *Christian Man's Calling*, 1:158.

in fear and faith. When we hear God's precepts in fear, the result is obedience. When we hear God's promises in faith, the result is hope. Every recorded work of God serves to strengthen our faith, and every recorded promise of God serves to strengthen our hope.

Third, in terms of our "behavior" after reading Scripture, we "practice."[12] That is to say, we obey; we respond practically to what Scripture teaches. Swinnock also asserts that we must "pray" after reading Scripture, to ask God to bless His Word to us.[13] "After the seed is sown," writes Swinnock, "the influence of heaven must cause it to spring up and ripen, or otherwise there will be no harvest."[14] God is the source of all knowledge, but He imparts knowledge to us through means. We *study*, meaning we inquire into the meaning of God's Word. We *observe*, meaning we compare God's curses and promises with His works of providence. We *consider*, meaning we seek to reflect the light of truth into our souls. This approach to Scripture is the means by which the Holy Spirit illuminates our spiritual eyes.

Swinnock also stresses the importance of Scripture meditation, which is closely related to reading. When Swinnock speaks of meditation, he isn't referring to the mere reading and studying of Scripture, but the *purposeful* reading and studying of Scripture. Its goal is the internalization of God's Word, and it involves *musing* and *mulling* over the biblical text, whereby the truth of God's Word grips the understanding, affections, and will. Swinnock defines it as "a serious applying of the mind to some sacred subject, till the affections be warmed and quickened, and the resolution heightened and strengthened thereby, against what is evil, and for that which is good."[15]

He encourages us to "retire out of the world's company, to converse with the Word of God."[16] He believes this "conversing" (or meditation) is essential because it functions like fire to water.[17]

---

12. Swinnock, *Christian Man's Calling*, 1:166.
13. Swinnock, *Christian Man's Calling*, 1:163.
14. Swinnock, *Christian Man's Calling*, 1:163.
15. Swinnock, *Christian Man's Calling*, 2:425.
16. Swinnock, *Christian Man's Calling*, 2:429.
17. Swinnock, *Christian Man's Calling*, 1:249.

Water is naturally cold, but fire makes it hot, causing it to boil. Likewise, our hearts are naturally cold, but meditation makes them hot, causing them to "boil with love" for God and His Word. For Swinnock, therefore, Scripture meditation is how what's known in the head can seep down into the heart. He declares, "The spring of this knowledge may be in the head, and its rise in the understanding; but it slides down into the heart, breaks out into the life, and so flows along in the channel of grace and holiness, till at last it loses itself in the ocean of glory."[18] In short, meditation is the bridge that spans the gulf between theoretical and practical knowledge.

For Swinnock, this is the way to grow in godliness. As we struggle with sin, we face a constant dilemma. It arises from our knowledge of two truths. First, we know sin feels good. Second, we know sin displeases God. When we face temptation, we act upon one of those two truths. Which one? The answer is determined by which of the two is most attractive to us at that particular moment. For that reason, a large part of the duty of sanctification is seeking to make sin unattractive to us. For Swinnock, this is done through meditation. It opens the door between the head and the heart, whereby the Holy Spirit makes deep impressions upon our affections. He cultivates love for God, thereby making sin repugnant to us. Swinnock declares, "O reader, be confident of this, the more you know of the excellencies of God, the more you will prize His Son, submit to His Spirit, crucify the flesh, condemn the world, fear to offend Him, study to please Him, the more holy you will be in all manner of conversation."[19]

This is pivotal for pastors. Our ministries are shaped by the condition of our hearts. Whatever rules our hearts controls our ministries. For this reason, we must seek to be "nourished up in the words of faith and of good doctrine" (1 Tim. 4:6). Metaphorically, the expression "nourished up" means to digest inwardly. The verb is a present participle, indicating an ongoing process. In short, we must continually feed upon God's Word.

---

18. Swinnock, *Christian Man's Calling*, 1:373.
19. Swinnock, *Christian Man's Calling*, 3:156.

SEVEN

A Tender Mother

I desire to be tenderly disposed toward all the souls under my charge. May I esteem their worth and unchangeable condition in the next world. Lord, what a melting heart should I have toward them, when I consider that they will spend eternity in either heaven or hell. My Savior was a faithful and merciful High Priest. He had compassion on the multitude when they had nothing to eat. He refused to send them away empty, lest they faint in the wilderness. Oh, that I had that kind of pity toward souls! Lord, when I behold wounded, bleeding, dying souls, let my eyes affect my heart with sorrow. May I seek Thy blessing upon my diligent efforts for their recovery. Make me such a tender and affectionate mother that I patiently bear their offenses. May I willingly bear the burden of instructing my children. Although some people nurse children for the love of wages, may I nurse my children for the wages of love. Let all my actions toward them flow from sincere affection. May all my counsels and comforts, even my rod of reproof, be dipped in honey. When I am rebuking them for sin, and frightening them from sin with the fear of the unquenchable fire, let all my words be dipped in this sweet syrup of love. May they know that my anger against their sins proceeds from a tender love for their souls.

Many years ago, I witnessed something I would like to forget—a face-slapping, eye-gouging, hair-pulling confrontation between two "believers" in a church where I happened to be the guest preacher. (No, the confrontation had nothing to do with my sermon.) Was it a rare display of animosity? Thankfully, yes. Was it a rare attitude of heart? Sadly, no. The *spirit* of envy, malice, and selfishness—which gave rise to that unfortunate confrontation—is all too common among us. While far more subtle than any public "smackdown," it's just as damaging. It destroys relationships, divides churches, and dishonors Christ. It's nowhere more damaging than in the context of pastoral ministry.[1]

In the above quote, Swinnock prays, "I desire to be tenderly disposed toward all the souls under my charge." He asks God to fill him with "sincere affection" for his people. We have a wonderful example of such affection in the apostle Paul. During his second missionary journey, he visits the city of Thessalonica (Acts 17). In response to his preaching, many people are saved. But some of the Jews cause trouble, and so Paul leaves Thessalonica and travels to Berea. His enemies follow him and cause more trouble. And so Paul leaves Berea and travels to Athens.

After his departure from the region, the Jews question Paul's motives and methods in an attempt to discourage the young church. Paul feels the need to defend his ministry—after all, the gospel is at stake. Therefore, he writes to the church: "For you yourselves, brethren, know our entrance in unto you, that it was not in vain" (1 Thess. 2:1). The term "vain" literally means *empty*. In effect, Paul says, "That isn't how I ministered among you!" He defends his ministry, reminding them of how he preached and lived while among them.

To begin with, he describes his preaching of the gospel, making two key points. First, he says he was bold in conflict: "But even after that we had suffered before, and were shamefully entreated, as ye know, at Philippi, we were bold in our God to speak unto you the gospel of God with much contention" (v. 2). Second, he says he was sincere in motive: "For our exhortation was not of deceit, nor

---

1. For a helpful treatment of this subject, see Alexander Strauch, *Leading with Love* (Littleton, Colo.: Lewis and Roth, 2006).

of uncleanness, nor in guile" (v. 3). In other words, Paul's ministry wasn't marked by error, impurity, or deception. It was marked by sincerity—a desire to please God (vv. 4–6).

Paul proceeds to describe how he lived among the Thessalonians: "But we were gentle among you, even as a nurse cherisheth her children: so being affectionately desirous of you, we were willing to have imparted unto you, not the gospel of God only, but also our own souls, because ye were dear unto us" (vv. 7–8). Later in the same chapter, he again expresses his feelings for the Thessalonian believers. He's in Corinth—a long way from Thessalonica. He's afraid these believers might assume he has forgotten them; hence, he wants them to understand four things about his absence from them.

First, his absence is *costly*: "being taken from you" (v. 17). This is the only verse in the New Testament, where we find the verb *aporphanizo* (to be taken). It's the origin of our English word *orphan*. Here, Paul likens himself to a child, who has lost his parents. Second, his absence is *temporary*: "for a short time" (v. 17). He makes it clear that he intends to return to Thessalonica as soon as he can. Third, his absence is *bodily*: "in presence, not in heart" (v. 17). Despite the distance between them, he still loves them. He's thinking about them and praying for them. Fourth, his absence is *involuntary*: "we…endeavored the more abundantly to see your face with great desire…but Satan hindered us" (vv. 17–18). Paul makes it clear that the circumstances which prevent him from returning to Thessalonica are beyond his control. In all this, Paul's "sincere affection" for the Thessalonian believers is clearly evident.

If we're to follow Paul's example, we must rid ourselves of all that threatens our love for our people. One of the most serious threats arises from *envy*. Jonathan Edwards describes envy as "a disposition natural in men, who love to be uppermost." He adds, "This disposition is directly crossed, when they see others above them."[2] There are two important components to Edwards's definition. First, the desire to be "uppermost" is a natural disposition; we all desire to be honored,

---

2. Edwards, *Charity and Its Fruits*, 112.

esteemed, and admired. Second, envy is experienced when others cross our desire to be "uppermost." If we fail to mortify it, then malice and bitterness take hold. They fester. Eventually, we strike out.

We see it in the case of Cain and Abel. God was pleased with Abel's sacrifice, but not with Cain's. Cain was envious—his desire to be uppermost was crossed: "Cain was very wroth, and his countenance fell" (Gen. 4:5). As a result, he killed his brother with his own hands. We see it again in the case of Joseph and his brothers. Joseph had several dreams showing that his brothers would bow down to him some day. The brothers were envious—their desire to be uppermost was crossed: "And they hated him yet more for his dreams, and for his words" (Gen. 37:8). Most of them wanted to kill him, but they settled for selling him into slavery. We see it again in the case of David and Saul. The women sang, "Saul hath slain his thousands, and David his ten thousands." Saul hated it. He was envious—his desire to be uppermost was crossed: "And Saul eyed David from that day and forward" (1 Sam. 18:9). As a result, he tried to kill him.

If left unchecked, envy always spawns murderous intent. It always lashes out (in one way or another) against what we perceive to threaten our desire "to be uppermost." In the context of the church, few things are more corrosive. In the context of pastoral ministry, few things are more destructive.

Another serious threat to loving our people is *anger*. According to Jonathan Edwards, there are four "occasions" when anger is sinful: in its nature, occasion, objective, and measure.[3] First, it's sinful in its "nature" when it's an expression of pride or frustration. Let's imagine I'm stuck in traffic on the highway. I'm late for an appointment, and I become angry. My anger in such a situation is an expression of frustration.

Second, anger is sinful in its "occasion" when it's based on an error in judgment—a false perception. A friend once shared with me how upset he had become when he returned to his campsite and discovered his cooler missing. He was certain that someone at the

---

3. Edwards, *Charity and Its Fruits*, 187–96.

next campsite had taken it, so he bolted angrily through the woods toward the next campsite. Along the way, he heard the sound of someone (or something) shaking a cooler. He veered to the right, following the sound, and discovered a bear shaking his water cooler! We often err in our judgment. We misunderstand people's words and actions, and based on our misunderstanding, we become angry.

Third, anger is sinful in its "objective" when it's marked by a loss of control; that is, it oversteps the bounds of reason. I'm trying to make an appointment and am put on hold for ten minutes; I become angry and start pounding the wall with my fist. How does that help? It doesn't. It's irrational—beyond the bounds of reason.

Fourth, anger is sinful in its "measure" when it's out of proportion to its cause. Simply put, we go overboard in our response. Such anger will quickly strain the deepest of relationships—undermining confidence, testing patience, and subverting love. It will quickly ruin marriages, friendships, churches, and ministries.

As pastors, we must mortify in us all that disrupts "sincere affection" for our people. In 2003, a young man was hiking in a remote canyon in Utah when his right arm somehow became pinned under a boulder. He couldn't free it, and he couldn't move the boulder. He had some food and water, and so he waited for help to arrive. But after five days, he realized that no one was going to find him. At this point, he was forced to make a choice. He could die, or he could remove his arm. He did the unimaginable. With a dull pocketknife, he cut through flesh, tendon, muscle, and bone. Having freed himself, he then walked out of the canyon.

Figuratively, that's how we must deal with our sin—with the envy, anger, and whatever else that threatens our love for our people. The starting point for this radical surgery is the gospel. If we want to love others more, we must love God more. "But God commendeth his love toward us, in that, while we were yet sinners, Christ died for us" (Rom. 5:8).

Because of God's love, Christ was condemned so that we might be justified; punished so that we might be pardoned; cursed so that we might be blessed; wounded so that we might be healed; and forsaken so that we might be accepted. God's love isn't a trickling brook but a roaring river. When we abound in His love, we abound in love for others. We minister with "sincere affection." We "put on charity, which is the bond of perfectness" (Col. 3:14). And the church becomes a family of believers characterized by compassion, kindness, humility, meekness, and patience (Col. 3:12).

EIGHT

A Courageous Soldier

As a sworn soldier of the Lord of hosts, I wish that—when I experience trials and tribulations, and face danger and death—I might not forsake my Captain, but "endure hardness, as a good soldier of Jesus Christ" (2 Tim. 2:3). When I first enlisted, I understood that His army encounters grievous hardships and various hazards. I understood that to preach the gospel is, as Martin Luther says, to attract the hatred of the whole world. The enemy aims his greatest artillery at the walls of the church—the ministers of the Word. When I signed my name as a volunteer, I promised to live and die in this conflict. Because the enemies are numerous and the attacks are perilous, will I—like Peter—deny my righteous cause and disown my glorious Captain? Lord, let me die with Thee rather than deny Thee! Enable me through Thy strength to be ready to be bound and to die for Thy name's sake. My only safety is to keep close to my Savior. If I flee out of cowardliness, I can expect martial law. "If any man draw back, my soul shall have no pleasure in him" (Heb. 10:38). If I—like Jonah—were to run from Thy presence, unwilling to deliver an unwelcome message, I would expect a storm to follow me—either the waves would swallow me up or the whale would swallow me down. If the service of my God is not the best, then why did I choose it? If it is the best, then why would I leave it? My cause is good: I fight against sin and Satan. My crown is better: an eternal crown of glory. My Captain is best: He watches over me, goes before me, and fights for me. He leads me into this trial. He will not—like the devil and the world—leave me in the lurch, but deliver me—either on earth or in heaven. Lord, whatever dirt of calumny is thrown in my face, or whatever dart of cruelty is stuck in my body, for keeping the Word of Thy patience in an hour of temptation, enable me to remain steadfast. Let me not count my life as dear. May I finish my course with joy. May I finish the ministry, which Thou hast entrusted to me, in order "to testify the gospel of the grace of God" (Acts 20:24).

In one scene of *Fiddler on the Roof*, the main character, Tevye, says to God: "I know, I know. We are your chosen people. But, once in a while, can't you choose someone else?" I wonder how many pastors have expressed a similar sentiment: "Can't you choose someone else?" As Swinnock acknowledges, "to preach the gospel is…to attract the hatred of the whole world." The world has no problem with a Christ who is portrayed as a coach, teacher, counselor, or humanitarian. But it won't tolerate a Christ who denounces sin. By extension, it won't tolerate those who preach the gospel. Swinnock knows it. He also knows he's weak. But he doesn't want to turn back in the face of danger or fall back in the hour of temptation. His prayer, therefore, is that he might "endure hardness, as a good soldier of Jesus Christ."

Here, Swinnock quotes 2 Timothy 2:3. The context of this letter from Paul to Timothy is significant. As Timothy ministers in the city of Ephesus, he struggles with ministerial discouragement. Why? There are a host of reasons. For starters, he's experiencing opposition and surrounded by doctrinal defection. Gnostic philosophies have a stranglehold on the people, who are unable to discern between truth and error and are losing their appetite for God's Word.

Timothy may also be experiencing frustration. He's dumbfounded by people's spiritual apathy. There's rampant carnality within the church but little growth so that the losses far surpass the gains. It's also possible Timothy is experiencing confusion. He's convinced he's in over his head and ill-equipped to deal with the mounting problems. He feels as though he's navigating a minefield.

Timothy could possibly be experiencing isolation. He's perplexed by an increasing feeling of loneliness, and he has little support in the church. His one source of support (Paul) is in prison, awaiting execution. What will happen once Paul is gone? What will it mean for the church? What will it mean for him? His ministerial duties have left him with few other friends.

For whatever reasons, Timothy is struggling with ministerial discouragement, and he's on the verge of walking away. "Can't you choose someone else?" Does any of this sound familiar? Ministerial discouragement is the chief reason pastors leave the ministry. They arrive at a point where they're convinced the cost far outweighs the reward.

At times like these, we must take to heart Paul's admonition to Timothy: "endure hardness, as a good soldier of Jesus Christ." In a word, Paul invites Timothy to *suffer* with him. That seems like a bizarre statement. Can you imagine a mission organization with this motto: *Come, suffer with us.* How many recruits would it attract? Can you imagine a Bible college with this motto: *Come, suffer with us.* How many students would it attract? Can you imagine a local church with this motto: *Come, suffer with us.* How many members would it attract? To the modern mind, Paul's invitation seems absurd.

Yet set in the context of the entire letter, it's evident that Paul's admonition is anything but absurd. Earlier, he reminds Timothy that "God hath not given us the spirit of fear; but of power, and of love, and of a sound mind" (2 Tim. 1:7). Regrettably, client-centered therapy is all the rage today. It rests on this basic assumption: we possess in ourselves all the resources we need to resolve our problems. In actual fact, we don't. To calm Timothy's fear, Paul doesn't point him to some secret source of inner strength. On the contrary, he points him away from himself to God.

He reminds him that God has given us the Holy Spirit, who is a Spirit of power in that He gives us the strength to serve. He's the Spirit of love in that He gives us the motivation to serve, and the Spirit of self-control in that He gives us the discipline to serve. That reality speaks of possessing and protecting, guarding and guiding, cherishing and challenging, supporting and sustaining. We can engage in pastoral ministry with this truth ringing in our ears: "Not by might, nor by power, but by my Spirit, saith the LORD of hosts" (Zech. 4:6).

Pastoral ministry is often discouraging. Yet Christ commands us (pastors included) to take up our cross (an instrument of torture) and follow Him (Luke 9:23). The cross is how God saves us. The cross is also a demonstration of how God works through us. That is to say, He works through suffering. As Paul declares, "[I] rejoice in my sufferings for you, and fill up that which is behind of the afflictions of Christ in my flesh for his body's sake, which is the church" (Col. 1:24). Regarding this verse, John Flavel remarks:

> He suffered once in…His own person, as Mediator. These sufferings are complete and full, and in that sense He suffers no more. He suffers also in…His church and members, thus He still suffers in the sufferings of every saint for His sake. And though these sufferings in His mystical body are not equal to the other, either…in their weight and value, nor yet designed…for the same use and purpose, to satisfy by their proper merit, offended justice; nevertheless they are truly reckoned the sufferings of Christ, because the Head suffers when the members do.[1]

Here, Flavel makes clear that Paul isn't suggesting that something is lacking in Christ's atoning work. The term "affliction" (*thlipsis*) is never used in reference to Christ's suffering on the cross; rather, it's used to describe the tribulations that He encountered during the course of His life. He experienced opposition, persecution, and rejection in this world. He continues to do so through His mystical body, the church.

As far as Paul is concerned, it's a joy to fill up what is "behind" (or lacking) in Christ's afflictions. Suffering isn't just the way Christ triumphs; it's the way we triumph. Weakness isn't just the way Christ conquers; it's the way we conquer. "When you feel your weakness and ineptitude, and as you are conscious of the forces that are set

---

1. Flavel, *Method of Grace*, 2:36–37.

against you," writes Martyn Lloyd-Jones, "remember that He, the Head of the body to which you belong, is at the right hand of God, that all authority and power is in His hands, controlling the universe and the cosmos, that He is Head over all things. He can direct everything, the wind and the storm, the rain and the sunshine; He can order all things, and is doing so—for you!"[2]

---

2. Martyn Lloyd-Jones, *Studies in the Sermon on the Mount: Volumes 1–2* (Grand Rapids: Eerdmans, 1962), 1:444.

NINE

A Prudent Preacher

The minister's principal work is the preaching of the gospel, with which he undermines and overturns the stronghold of sin and the kingdom of darkness. Therefore, I wish that I might prepare for this work diligently, handle this weapon carefully, and deliver this message soberly, in a manner that is most for my God's glory and my people's good—not with the enticing words of man's wisdom, but in the demonstration of the Spirit's power.

Prayerfully
To this end, I desire that all my sermons might be, like Monica's son,[1] children of many tears and prayers, and thereby unlikely to perish. Martin Luther says, "Whoever prays hard studies hard." Lord, may all my sermons be heaven-born. May they drop down on my people like rain on the grass. Let prayer be the key that opens the mysteries of Christ to me. Let prayer be the key that locks them safe inside me. Let prayer open and close all my reading, writing, and preparing. Let prayer begin and conclude all my sermons. In every sermon, I preach my beloved neighbors into eternal burnings or eternal pleasures. Oh, how I should pray for my preaching and before my preaching!

Passionately
I also wish that I might preach every sermon to my own heart before I preach it to others, so that—preaching feelingly—I might

---

1. Monica was Augustine's mother, who famously prayed for her son's conversion for many years.

preach effectually. May the Word come naturally, like milk from the mother's breasts, to nourish my children. Why would I plead God's cause without having a personal interest in it? Oh, let me be like the doctor, who takes the same remedy he prescribes to his patients.

Purely
I desire that I might never play the huckster with God's Word—adulterating it with my own additions. May I receive from the Lord what I deliver to others. May I feed all under my charge with the sincere milk of the Word, so that they might grow. As an ambassador, may I keep close to my instructions. As a builder, may I set every stone in God's temple by the line and rule of His Word. As a doctor, may I never experiment upon my people's souls, but prescribe those tested and approved remedies, which the great Physician has entrusted to me.

Plainly
Because my work is to touch and pierce my people's hearts, and not to tickle and please their ears, I wish that I might preach a crucified Savior in a crucified style. May I not paint my sermons with a showy display of words, but employ all plainness, stooping to their lowest capacity. May I be "made all things to all men, that I might by all means save some" (1 Cor. 9:22). I am a foreigner to my people, if I preach to them in an unknown language. I starve their souls, if I give them meat that they can never digest. Let me not read commentaries as the butterfly goes to the flower to gild her wings, but as the bee goes to the flower to gather honey to supply her young. Lord, let me never be guilty of painting the windows, thereby hindering the light of Thy glorious gospel from shining powerfully into the hearts of men and women.

Prudently
My prayer is that I might not strengthen the hands of the ungodly nor sadden the hearts of the godly, but distinguish between the vile and the precious, and preach to each accordingly. May I give milk to babes and meat to adults. May I order my prescriptions in a manner that is suitable to their constitutions. May I use the

needle of the law to make way for the thread of the gospel. May I lead my people—like Jacob his flock—as they are able to bear it. And may I teach my people—as Christ His disciples—as they are best able to hear it.

Powerfully
Oh, that I might not only preach prudently, but also powerfully. May my sermons be delivered, not as prologues to a play, but as the message of a herald with all seriousness and fervency, containing conditions of life and death. The Word is a hammer, but it will never break the stony heart if it is not brought to bear. What is preached coldly is heard carelessly. Lord, let me not—like the moon—give light without heat. Cause me to lift up my voice like a trumpet to give—like fire—heat as well as light. May I be consumed with zeal for Thy house. May I beseech poor souls to be happy, as if I were begging for my life. May I preach so successfully that I might produce much fruit.

Swinnock believes "the minister's principal work is the preaching of the gospel." This high regard for preaching accounts for his many "wishes." For example, he desires to preach from the heart; he desires to preach "a crucified Savior in a crucified style"; and he desires to preach seriously and fervently. In the midst of his list, Swinnock includes this interesting request: "May I use the needle of the law to make way for the thread of the gospel." In this single phrase, he touches on one of the most important aspects of preaching—leading people to the gospel by way of the law.

Why is this so important? In short, people must perceive their need of Christ before they will rest in Christ. In *The Pilgrim's Progress*, John Bunyan provides a powerful illustration of this reality. Christian and Pliable set out from the City of Destruction for the Celestial City. Soon after, they veer from the path, and fall into the Slough of Despond. Pliable is so dejected and disappointed that he decides to return home. Why? The answer is found in what he says to Christian while they're struggling in the Slough: "Is this the happiness you have told me all this while of?"[2] This question is revealing. It shows that Christian and Pliable embark on the journey for very different reasons. Pliable's reason is *carnal*. He doesn't have any sense of his sin. He doesn't have any burden on his back. In a word, he's motivated by self-interest. When the way becomes difficult, and his perceived interests aren't met, he becomes disillusioned. Unsurprisingly, he turns back. But Christian's reason is *spiritual*. He's conscious of his sin—the burden on his back—and is looking for someone who is able to save him from his sin. He hungers and thirsts after righteousness, and nothing will deter him from his pursuit.

We only believe in Christ, when we're convinced we need Him. That's what Swinnock has in mind when he prays, "May I use the needle of the law to make way for the thread of the gospel." But how exactly does this work in preaching?

First, we preach the law, in order to produce a *sight of sin*. When we preach, we compel people to examine themselves in the light of God's law. Why? Paul tells us: "I had not known sin, but by the law: for I had not known lust, except the law had said, 'Thou shalt not covet'" (Rom. 7:7). Through the tenth commandment, Paul realized that sin isn't primarily concerned with deeds, but with desires. In addition, he realized that his desires are as damnable as his deeds. Until that moment, he knew the law theoretically, but he didn't know it experimentally. By the Holy Spirit's work through the law, he came to know his sin.

This pivotal role of the law in revealing sin is evident in Christ's conversation with the rich ruler in Mark 10. This young man approaches Christ, asking, "What shall I do that I may inherit eternal life?" Christ responds by quoting six commandments from the Decalogue. The man claims, "Master, all these have I observed from my youth." Christ replies, "One thing thou lackest: go thy way, sell

---

2. John Bunyan, *The Pilgrim's Progress* (Uhrichsville, Ohio: Barbour, 1985), 8.

whatsoever thou hast, and give to the poor, and thou shalt have treasure in heaven" (v. 21).

What's Christ doing here? He isn't suggesting that the rich ruler can *do* something in order to inherit eternal life; rather, He's correcting the man's misunderstanding of the law. The man thinks he's able to be justified by the law. Christ challenges his misunderstanding of the function of the law by sending him to the tenth commandment: "Go thy way, sell whatsoever thou hast, and give to the poor." The rich ruler loves his wealth—he's covetous. The implications are obvious. If he's covetous, then he's an idolater. If he's an idolater, then he's guilty of breaking the first commandment: "Thou shalt have no other gods before me" (Ex. 20:3). Christ is showing the rich ruler that he hasn't kept the law, and that he can't keep the law. It doesn't exist to tell us what we *can* do, but what we *can't* do. That's how we preach the law.

Second, we preach the law, in order to cultivate a *sorrow for sin*. Christ declares, "Blessed are the poor in spirit: for theirs is the kingdom of heaven" (Matt. 5:3). Poverty of spirit is an attitude before God that arises from a proper self-perception. We perceive our sin in light of God's law. As a result, we recognize that we're without moral virtues adequate to commend ourselves to God. As a result, we're aware of our utter dependence upon God's grace. This awareness of utter nothingness is exemplified in Paul's experience. He writes, "For I was alive without the law once: but when the commandment came, sin revived, and I died" (Rom. 7:9).

Here, Paul describes life and death in relative terms. There was a time when he was "alive without the law," meaning he lacked any experimental knowledge of it. Without that knowledge, he thought all was well with his soul. He says of himself, "Touching the righteousness which is in the law, blameless" (Phil. 3:6). However, the time came when Paul "died." Why? The law arrived home, and sin became alive. In other words, the law revealed and provoked his sin. He saw God's righteousness. As a result, he saw the depths of his own depravity. It killed him; that is, it made him poor in spirit.

Third, we preach the law, in order to nurture a *desire for Christ*. When we're poor in spirit, we grasp that we're beyond all hope of attaining salvation on the basis of our righteousness. We realize we deserve God's wrath. This isn't a despair that arises from any doubt concerning God's mercy, but from our own inability. In other words, we despair of saving ourselves. Have you ever seen the finish to a marathon or triathlon? Many of the athletes collapse across the finish line. Why? They're exhausted—every ounce of energy is spent. That's how we feel when we truly understand the law. It requires us to do something we can't. It exhausts us.

When Christian first sets out for the Celestial City, he listens to the counsel of Mr. Worldly Wiseman.[3] Leaving the path, he heads for a high hill. Initially, the terrain is pleasant, but it soon begins to slope upward. Finally, it becomes a rock face. Christian is afraid it's going to fall on his head. His burden feels heavier than ever before. Where is he? He's at Mt. Sinai.

That's what the law does. It reveals our sin, compounds our guilt and shame, and condemns. In a word, it exhausts us. That's all it can do. When we're deeply affected in this manner, we become conscious of our sin, mindful of our burden, and aware of our need for a Savior. Exhausted, the Holy Spirit directs us to look elsewhere for assistance. Having learned the disease of our spiritual inability and impotency, we turn to Christ. He has fulfilled the law's demand and paid the law's penalty. We begin to desire Christ and His merits. We hunger and thirst after a righteousness that isn't our own—"the righteousness of God without the law" (Rom. 3:21). We rest in Christ, and our exhaustion is removed in Him. Our weariness is removed in Him. Our burden is removed in Him.

In our preaching, we must—as Swinnock says—"use the needle of the law to make way for the thread of the gospel." People must perceive their need for Christ in order to rest in Christ. Before people can be cured of a disease, they must first be convinced that it threatens their health and well-being. Once they're convinced of their condition, they recognize that they need a doctor to prescribe a remedy.

---

3. Bunyan, *The Pilgrim's Progress*, 15.

Similarly, they must recognize that they're *sick* (in danger from sin), before they'll seek Christ—the Physician of the soul. They must be "thirsty" before they'll drink of Christ (John 7:37). They must be "hungry" before they'll feed on Christ (John 6:35). They must be "weary and heavy laden" before they'll rest in Christ (Matt. 11:28–30). They must be like a "battered reed" (i.e., easy to break off) and a "smoldering wick" (i.e., easy to put out) before they'll turn to Christ (Matt. 12:20). There must be humiliation for sin before there will ever be faith in Christ because the language of faith is meaningless to those who remain unconvinced of their *need* for a Savior.

TEN

A Ceaseless Intercessor

I wish that my people might have so deep a share in my affection that I always make mention of them in my prayers. May my heart's desire, and my prayer to God in private and public, be for their salvation. Oh, let me daily confess their iniquity, mourn their misery, and cry mightily to God for mercy. Lord, let me prevail with Thee to speak to their hearts, and I will prevail with them to listen to Thee. May I be able to stand before Thee at the last day with courage, and say, "Behold, I and the children whom the LORD hath given me" (Isa. 8:18).

Don Carson asks, "What is the most urgent need in the church of the Western world today?" We could probably make quite a list. But Carson answers his own question as follows: "We need to know God better.... One of the foundational steps in knowing God, and one of the basic demonstrations that we do know God, is prayer—spiritual, persistent, biblically minded prayer."[1] As pastors, do we pray? Do we pray for our people? Swinnock feels the weight of this responsibility. He asks God to enlarge his love for his people, so that he might pray for them affectionately, regularly, and consistently. He adds, "Oh, let me daily confess their iniquity, mourn their misery, and cry mightily to God for mercy!"

---

1. Don Carson, *A Call to Spiritual Reformation: Priorities from Paul and His Prayers* (Grand Rapids: Baker, 1992), 11, 15–16.

What makes for effectual prayer? Christ is staying at Bethany. As He walks to Jerusalem, He passes the fig tree that He had cursed on a previous visit. He declares to His disciples: "Have faith in God. For verily I say to you, That whosoever shall say unto this mountain, Be thou removed, and be thou cast into the sea; and shall not doubt in his heart, but shall believe that those things which he saith shall come to pass; he shall have whatsoever he saith" (Mark 11:23). He then proceeds to teach them that mountain-moving prayer possesses two essential ingredients: faith and forgiveness.

The first essential ingredient is *faith*. Christ says, "What things soever ye desire, when ye pray, believe that ye receive them, and ye shall have them" (Mark 11:24). What does it mean to believe that we have received? Paul's statement, in Romans 4:18, is particularly helpful. He describes Abraham as believing against hope in hope. Please notice three facts. First, Abraham believed. What did he believe? He believed God's promise to give him a son. Second, Abraham believed "against hope." In other words, he considered his age and Sarah's barrenness, and he realized that God's promise was hopeless—humanly speaking. Third, Abraham believed "in hope." He considered God's power and faithfulness, and he realized that God's promise was an absolute certainty. What was the result? Abraham was "fully persuaded that, what he had promised, he was able also to perform" (Rom. 4:21).

In short, to believe that we have received is to be fully convinced that God is able to do what He has promised to do. That's another way of saying that to pray in faith is to pray according to God's will as revealed in His Word (1 John 5:2–3). As Swinnock notes, "God's Word and will must be the rule of our prayers.... Divine precepts, what God commands us to act; divine promises, what God engages himself to do for us; and divine prophecies, what God has foretold will come to pass, are the bounds of our prayers. Whoever goes beyond these limits in his request wanders to his loss."[2]

To believe that we have received is to pray for obedience to submit to what God decrees. Job cries, "Naked came I out of my

---

2. Swinnock, *Christian Man's Calling*, 1:121.

mother's womb, and naked shall I return thither: the LORD gave, and the LORD hath taken away; blessed be the name of the LORD" (Job 1:21). Similarly, we pray that we might accept what God wills as what is best. When He wills sickness, sickness is better than health. When He wills weakness, weakness is better than strength. When He wills reproach, reproach is better than honor. When He wills poverty, poverty is better than wealth. When He wills persecution, persecution is better than peace. When He wills valleys, valleys are better than mountaintops. When He wills death, death is better than life. Do we struggle to believe and accept this? We must pray.

To believe that we have received is to pray for obedience to obey what God commands. Among other things, He commands us to love one another, abstain from what is evil, pursue righteousness, submit to those in authority over us, be patient and humble, love our spouse, share with those in need, make disciples, abstain from immorality, resist the evil one, be faithful stewards and diligent servants, worship Him, forgive one another, be strong, endure persecution, and love our neighbor. We can't do any of these things in our own strength. We can't obey in our own power. And so, we must pray.

To believe that we have received is to pray for obedience to cherish what God promises. William Gurnall comments, "Prayer is nothing but the promise reversed, or God's Word formed into an argument, and retorted by faith upon God again."[3] God promises to impart wisdom in the midst of trials and to give peace in all circumstances. He promises to forgive, when we confess our sins. He promises to never leave us nor forsake us and to abide in us. He promises to come for us, raise us from the dead, and crush the devil. He promises to build His church. He promises to work all things together for our good, complete the work He has started in us, and take us as His people. Do we live upon these promises? Do they impart strength when we're weak, joy when we're downcast, and hope when we're discouraged?

---

3. As quoted in I. D. E. Thomas, *A Puritan Golden Treasury* (Edinburgh: Banner of Truth, 2000), 210.

We must pray in faith, according to God's Word—not without a promise and not against a command. That means, in the words of John Calvin, "Faith grounded upon the Word is the mother of right prayer."[4]

The second ingredient of mountain-moving faith is *forgiveness*. Christ says, "And when ye stand praying, forgive, if ye have ought against any: that your Father also which is in heaven may forgive you your trespasses" (Mark 11:26). What does it mean to forgive? It means to withhold revenge, mortify anger, cultivate love, and render good. Why is forgiveness so important? An unwillingness to forgive destroys the closest of relationships and breaks the door to the heart, leaving it wide open for other sins to enter. An unwillingness to forgive prevents spiritual growth and maturity and reveals deep-rooted pride.

Finally, an unwillingness to forgive belittles God's grace as displayed in the gospel, as Christ teaches in this parable from Matthew 18. A servant owes a huge amount of money to his king; he can't pay it and pleads for mercy. The king forgives him his debt. But the same servant finds someone who owes him a small amount of money; the debtor can't pay and pleads for mercy. But the servant throws him into prison anyway. When the king hears of it, he's enraged and throws the servant into prison. Christ says, "So likewise shall my heavenly Father do also unto you, if ye from your hearts forgive not every one his brother their trespasses" (Matt. 18:35).

An unforgiving heart is a heart untouched by God's grace. Do you struggle to forgive someone who has criticized you? God has forgiven you for blaspheming His name. Do you struggle to forgive someone who has wronged you? God has forgiven you for disobeying His Word. Do you struggle to forgive someone who has abandoned you? God has forgiven you for abusing His glory. Do you struggle to forgive someone who has injured you? God has forgiven you for murdering His Son. Christ's point is that God's forgiveness makes us forgiving. Mercy experienced is mercy bestowed.

---

4. John Calvin, *Institutes of the Christian Religion*, ed. J. T. McNeill, trans. Ford Lewis Battles (Philadelphia: Westminster, 1960), 3.20.27.

These two—faith and forgiveness—are the marks of effectual prayer. But what exactly are we to request when we pray for our people? A. W. Pink remarks, "What [the apostle Paul] requested for the saints are the particular things which Christians in all ages are to especially desire, prize, and seek an increase of."[5] In other words, we find the content of our prayers in Paul's prayers. For example, he prays "that the God of our Lord Jesus Christ, the Father of glory, may give unto you the spirit of wisdom and revelation in the knowledge of him" (Eph. 1:17). William Hendriksen explains, "Paul asks that the addressed may receive a continually growing supply of wisdom and clear knowledge. Combine the two, and note that he is asking that the Ephesians be given deeper penetration into the meaning of the gospel and a clearer insight into the will of God for their lives, enabling them at all times to use the best means for the attainment of the highest goal, namely, the glory of God Triune."[6]

Two things are indispensable to vision: light and sight. The natural man lacks both. The Holy Spirit, therefore, must enlighten us. Paul wants the opening of our spiritual eyes to lead to the knowledge of three great truths: the hope of God's calling (v. 18), the assurance of our personal interest in the thing for which we hope; the riches of the glory of God's inheritance in the saints (v. 18), whereas the church doesn't exist for itself but for God's glory; and the surpassing greatness of God's power toward us who believe (v. 19).

Paul also prays "that Christ may dwell in your hearts by faith" (Eph. 3:17). The result of Christ's dwelling in our hearts is that we're "rooted and grounded in love." The word "rooted" suggests a tree; just as the earth is the source of sustenance for the tree, love is the source of sustenance for us. The word "grounded" suggests a building; just as the foundation provides stability to the building, love provides stability to us. In short, love should be the predominant element in our lives so that we're "able to comprehend with all the saints what is

---

5. A. W. Pink, *Gleanings from Paul: Studies in the Prayers of the Apostle* (Edinburgh: Banner of Truth, 2006), 303.

6. William Hendriksen, *The New Testament Commentary: Exposition of Ephesians* (Grand Rapids: Baker, 1987), 98.

the breadth, and length, and depth, and height; and to know the love of Christ, which passeth knowledge" (Eph. 3:18–19). With this verse, says Martyn Lloyd-Jones, "we find ourselves, as it were, upon the pinnacle of Christian truth. There is nothing higher than this."[7] To "comprehend" is to take a firm mental grasp of something—to gain a conceptual knowledge. We comprehend that God's love is boundless: its breadth is without boundary; its length is without end; its depth is without measure; and its height is without limit. To "know the love of Christ" is an experiential knowledge. Paul wants us to know the dimensions of God's love in our daily experience. When this happens, we're "filled with all the fullness of God" (v. 19).

Is that how we pray for our people? "I wish," says Swinnock, "that my people might have so deep a share in my affection that I always make mention of them in my prayers." Are our prayers *humble*? "Prayer is one of our nearest approaches to God on this side of heaven. In it we speak to God mouth to mouth," Swinnock says. "Therefore, it must be poured out with much humility."[8] Are our prayers *hearty*? "God looks not so much to the elegancy of your prayers—how neat they are; nor to the geometry of your prayers—how long they are; but to the sincerity of your prayers—how hearty they are."[9] Are our prayers *fervent*? "When you are begging grace and purity, you should pray with earnestness. You must see how destructive sin is to your precious soul, and how offensive it is to the jealous, just, and almighty God. You must see your absolute necessity of holiness, without which you can never see God."[10] Are our prayers *constant*? "A Christian's prayer may have an intermission, but never a cessation."[11]

---

7. Martyn Lloyd-Jones, *The Unsearchable Riches of Christ: An Exposition of Ephesians 3* (Grand Rapids: Baker, 2003), 3:205.
8. Swinnock, *Christian Man's Calling*, 1:123.
9. Swinnock, *Christian Man's Calling*, 1:124–25.
10. Swinnock, *Christian Man's Calling*, 1:126.
11. Swinnock, *Christian Man's Calling*, 1:129.

ELEVEN

A Patient Instructor

As they sail along in the sea of this world, the small keels of children are quickly overturned when they meet with strong winds, if they are not ballasted with the principles of the Word of God. For this reason, I pray that I might be a diligent instructor of the young, and a faithful teacher of the simple. May I season new vessels—through God's help—with the precious water of life, so that they retain their savor into their old age. May the younger among my people know the Scriptures, "which are able to make thee wise unto salvation through faith which is in Christ Jesus" (2 Tim. 3:15).

"Weebles wobble, but they don't fall down." Does that little ditty bring back memories? If so, you must be over forty. If not, let me fill you in on a cultural phenomenon from the 1970s. Weebles were little egg-shaped plastic figurines, weighted in such a way that—when knocked over—they would bounce back. No matter how hard or how often they wobbled, they always returned to their default position. So what's my point? Simply this: when it comes to doctrine, we're not unlike Weebles—we have a default position.

When left to ourselves, we naturally gravitate to error. Why? There are numerous reasons. We're attracted to the carnal and sensual, meaning we're drawn to whatever appeals to our senses. We're enamored with novelty and, therefore, always on the lookout for the spectacular and sensational. We're susceptible to relativism—the notion that everyone is entitled to his version of the truth. We're susceptible to mysticism—the notion that truth is discovered through private intuition. We're susceptible to pragmatism—the notion that we determine the value of truth by its perceived usefulness to us. And on it goes.

For many of us, the greatest danger isn't always the open denial of doctrines that are essential to the Christian faith. The danger is relegating these doctrines to the periphery of the Christian faith, whereby they become inconsequential. In other words, it's determining the importance of these doctrines on the basis of how useful they seem to us. When that happens, we don't become heretics in confession, but in life. It's possible to hold verbally to a doctrinally sound confession of faith yet live in such a manner that we become functional heretics.

Our people are susceptible to doctrinal subterfuge, if they aren't (in Swinnock's words) "ballasted with the principles of the Word of God." Ballast is what a ship needs to stay upright; without weight to stabilize it, the ship will tip over on its side and won't be able to withstand wind and waves. Our people need ballast; otherwise, they'll be "quickly overturned when they meet with strong winds." This is part of the reason why Paul says that an elder must hold "fast the faithful word as he hath been taught, that he may be able by sound doctrine both to exhort, and to convince the gainsayers" (Titus 1:9). Here, Paul makes clear that teaching has two essential components. In positive terms, it involves instructing in sound doctrine. In negative terms, it involves refuting those who contradict sound doctrine. These two responsibilities encapsulate a pastor's primary calling.

In *The Pilgrim's Progress*, John Bunyan points to the importance of this ministry by emphasizing the pivotal role played by Interpreter in helping Christian on his way to the Celestial City.[1] In the House of the Interpreter, Christian sees various people, pictures, parlors, and palaces. But he can't make any sense of it and needs Interpreter's

---

1. Bunyan, *Pilgrim's Progress*, 25–33.

help. At this point of the narrative, Bunyan is emphasizing the need for sound interpretation. Why? There are two reasons.

First, sound interpretation is necessary for *understanding accurately*. Christian doesn't understand what he sees until Interpreter explains it. Similarly, for many Christians today, much of Scripture is opaque until interpreted. As pastors, our role is to provide clarity—to expound Scripture. We must assume the role of Philip, who asks the Ethiopian eunuch: "Understandest thou what thou readest?" To which, the eunuch replies, "How can I, except some man should guide me?" (Acts 8:30–31). That's what our people need. They need us to guide them into God's Word and unfold it before them so that they're able to feed upon it more fully.

Second, sound interpretation is necessary for *walking faithfully*. By the time Christian arrives at the House of Interpreter, he's saved, yet he isn't saved. He has left the City of Destruction, but he hasn't arrived at the Celestial City. In other words, he's on a journey, and Interpreter's role is essential to Christian's safe sojourn. Christian needs instruction so that he will be equipped to navigate the perilous waters ahead of him. Likewise, we must provide instruction for our people so that they will be "perfect, thoroughly furnished unto all good works" (2 Tim. 3:17).

Paul writes, "Study to show thyself approved unto God, a workman that needeth not to be ashamed, rightly dividing the word of truth" (2 Tim. 2:15). In the ancient world, people used coins made of various metals. Some people would shave coins, collect the shavings, and make new ones. Money changers who refused to accept shaved coins were called *dokimos*—approved. That's the term Paul uses in this verse; we must study to show ourselves "approved." The expression "rightly dividing" is *orthotomeo*, the source of our English term *orthodox* and literally means to cut straight. Paul's point is that we must seek to be accurate in our interpretation of God's Word.

At any given moment, a local church is only one generation (at most) away from doctrinal heresy because our natural inclination is away from the truth. Just as a compass always points north, we naturally gravitate to error. And so we must heed Paul's command to Timothy: "charge some that they teach no other doctrine" (1 Tim. 1:3). The verb "charge" is a military term meaning to give strict orders, and by using this term, Paul makes it clear that this isn't the time for dialogue, but action. Why? False teaching threatens the gospel, and Paul's love for this church compels him to defend the gospel. Therefore, he urges Timothy to take a stand.

What dangers confront the church today? I see a number of troubling trends, the first being a deistic view of God. The philosophical/theological position known as "Deism" was popular in the 1700s. Deists believed in a God who made few demands on His creatures. Today, many evangelicals have adopted a similar view. They limit God's sovereignty; He has surrendered His rule to man's free will. They limit God's omnipotence; He has surrendered His infinite power to man's sentimental notion of unconditional love. They limit God's immutability; He has surrendered His unchangeableness to accommodate man's aspirations. In short, they've fashioned a god in their own image.

The second troubling trend is a therapeutic view of Christianity. In our society, the pursuit of happiness is interpreted to mean the pursuit of *self*, which means that human personality is to be discovered, modified, and cultivated. Evangelicalism has redefined itself accordingly. For evidence, we can look at the average Christian bookstore, where the vast majority of books are related to nurturing ourselves, resolving tensions, overcoming obstacles, etc. In the words of David Wells, we have "moved from a doctrinally framed faith the central concern of which was truth to a therapeutically constructed faith the central concern of which is psychological survival."[2]

The third troubling trend is a subjective view of spirituality. Generally speaking, there are four competing concepts of spirituality: paganism looks to nature; Roman Catholicism looks to sense; Quakerism looks to feeling; and Protestantism (traditionally defined) looks to God's Word. Today, there's a growing interest in spirituality. Sadly, this interest is focused on communion with God

---

2. Wells, *No Place for Truth*, 209.

via nature or sense or feeling. There's little interest in creeds and confessions, in truth and doctrine, in laborious biblical study, in tedious theological study, or in wrestling with difficult questions. The interest is mostly subjective.

The fourth troubling trend is a moralistic view of discipleship.[3] Many people believe in a God who is simply there when needed, but He isn't particularly involved in their lives, and He doesn't really make any demands upon them. He exists for the purpose of fostering their sense of personal peace and happiness, and anyone who suggests otherwise is conveniently dismissed as a legalist. They prefer a Christ who winks at materialism, embraces casual commitment, and accepts them just the way they are. They prefer a Christ who doesn't make any demands on them and wants them to be happy above all else. They prefer a Christ who doesn't expect them to forsake their closest ungodly relationships, or give away what they possess, or place themselves in dangerous situations. They don't want a Christ who calls them to self-denial, but self-fulfillment. The result is a lukewarm, compromising brand of Christianity.

If we're going to protect our people, we must warn them of the enemy. Have you ever heard of Pickett's charge? At the battle of Gettysburg, General Lee ordered a charge across an open field toward what he assumed was the weakest section in the Union line. He was sorely mistaken; General Meade was waiting on the higher ground. In less than an hour, thousands of Confederate soldiers were dead, and many more were injured. How could General Lee make such a mistake? He underestimated his enemy. As pastors, we dare not underestimate our enemy. He's a snake, seeking to deceive God's people (2 Cor. 11:3); a wolf, seeking to destroy God's sheep (Matt. 10:16; John 10:12); a lion, seeking to devour God's children (1 Peter 5:8).

If we're going to protect our people, we must warn them of the danger. Warning signs serve an important function. There's a tidal

---

3. For more on this subject, see Jonathan Lunde, *Following Jesus, the Servant King: A Biblical Theology of Covenantal Discipleship* (Grand Rapids: Zondervan, 2010).

island off the northeast coast of England, called Lindisfarne, where the causeway is flooded twice per day. When the tide is out, it's possible to walk or drive across the causeway to the island. At different points along the way, there are refuge boxes with warning signs: "If you see water, climb up." The tide comes in so quickly that there's no time to make it to the other side of the causeway, and each year, at least one car is stranded in the tide because the driver ignored the warning signs. We ignore warning signs to our peril.

The same is true in the context of the church. As pastors, we must warn. Children are orally fixated, which is why they put everything in their mouths. For this reason, we teach children to discern what's harmful to them, and as they grow, they learn. If they reach sixteen years of age and are still putting marbles in their mouths, we know they aren't very mature. Similarly, in the context of the church, we must train our people to grow in discernment—the ability to judge between what's evil and good, true and false, right and wrong. We must provide ballast—what Swinnock calls "the principles of the Word of God."

TWELVE

A Discerning Judge

I wish that in the administration of the sacraments I might have an impartial regard to the fitness of my people, lest I set those precious seals of the covenant of grace before blanks. When it comes to the Lord's Supper, I do not want to partake of other men's sin, nor do I not want to be an instrument which furthers their eternal suffering. May I be tender and walk by the rule of Scripture. Oh, let me never pollute that sacred ordinance by giving it to profane persons. May I never be so prodigal of my dearest Savior's blood and body, as to give those holy things to dogs, and to cast those pearls before swine, who will trample them under their feet (Matt. 7:6). Oh, it is better for such scandalous sinners to be angry with me on earth on account of my wholesome severity than to curse me forever in hell on account of my foolish pity and soul-damning flattery!

Here, Swinnock expresses his desire to be "impartial" when it comes to judging the spiritual condition of his people. Naturally, he doesn't want to incur anyone's displeasure, yet he recognizes the significance of church discipline as a means by which the Holy Spirit brings sinners to repentance. Admittedly, when it comes to "other men's sin," it's far easier to overlook than confront, to ignore than rebuke, to disregard than discipline. Yet, God calls us to judge. Art Azurdia cautions, "Today the church faces a moral crisis within her own ranks. Her failure to take a strong stand against evil (even in her own midst), and her tendency to be more concerned about what is expedient than what is right, has robbed the church of biblical integrity and power."[1]

Similarly, Albert Mohler writes, "The decline of church discipline is perhaps the most visible failure of the contemporary church. No longer concerned with maintaining purity of confession or lifestyle, the contemporary church sees itself as a voluntary association of autonomous members, with minimal moral accountability to God, much less to each other."[2] One of the church's most urgent needs is to recapture the practice of biblical church discipline in order to fulfill its calling to convey God's holiness to the world. The Holy Spirit cultivates holiness among God's people through appointed means, what Swinnock calls "secret, private, and public duties."[3] These are "conduit-pipes whereby the water of life is derived from Christ in the hearts of Christians."[4] Among these means stands church discipline.

Now, I realize the expression "church discipline" creates a dilemma for most people as they think church discipline contradicts Christ's command: "Judge not, that ye be not judged" (Matt. 7:1). But what does Christ mean by this command? For starters, He isn't talking about *public denunciation*. At times, it's necessary to denounce the sins of leaders, churches, and countries. For example, Christ condemns the Pharisees as "whitewashed tombs" (Matt. 23:27) and Herod as a "fox" (Luke 13:32). He's warning of the danger of imitating or following their sinful example.

Secondly, Christ isn't talking about *private admonition*. As Christians, we're accountable for one another. If we see another Christian sin, we should admonish him. If another Christian sees

---

1. Art Azurdia, "Recovering the Third Mark of the Church," *Reformation and Revival* 3 (1994): 61–79.
2. Albert Mohler, "Church Discipline: The Missing Mark," *The Southern Baptist Journal of Theology* 4 (2000): 16.
3. Swinnock, *Fading of the Flesh*, 3:416.
4. Swinnock, *Christian Man's Calling*, 1:102.

us sin, he should admonish us. Of course, we should be very careful *how* we admonish one another, but the point is this: we're commanded to do so (Matt. 18:15).

Thirdly, Christ isn't talking about *church discipline*. In cases of scandalous sin, doctrinal heresy, or undisciplined behavior (accompanied by obstinacy), the church is to judge in order to ratify Christ's judgment. But many people object—some vehemently. In most cases, the cause of their objection is moral individualism; people don't believe anyone has the right to challenge their behavior. Regrettably, this thinking has infiltrated local churches, whereby many have become a loose association of casual relationships without any moral accountability. As a result, very few people tolerate church discipline; they simply hide behind their misinterpretation and misapplication of Christ's command: "Judge not, that ye be not judged."

So what's Christ really saying in this command? He's referring to an attitude of heart that bears two distinct marks. First, it's *hypercritical:* "For with what judgment ye judge, ye shall be judged: and with what measure ye mete, it shall be measured to you again" (Matt. 7:2). Here, Christ is rebuking those people who never have anything good to say. They're like rhinos in a china shop—they can't move without breaking something.

Second, this attitude of heart is *hypocritical:* "Thou hypocrite, first cast out the beam out of thine own eye; and then shalt thou see clearly to cast out the mote out of thy brother's eye" (v. 5). Hypocrisy is a double standard that arises from our desire to please men rather than God, which is what Christ rebukes here. He describes people who discern small faults in others while failing to discern great faults in themselves. David was guilty of this—on one occasion anyway. The prophet Nathan tells David a story about a wealthy man who stole a poor man's only lamb in order to feed a visitor (2 Sam. 12:1–7). Immediately, David identifies the man's sin, calls for justice, and passes sentence. Nathan didn't say, "You hypocrite!" But he could have because David was blind to his own sin, which was far worse than the theft of a lamb. He had fornicated with Bathsheba and orchestrated the death of her husband, Uriah. But hypocrisy is blinding. The hypocrite is able (and willing) to judge the sins of everyone but himself.

As William Perkins explains, we're hypocrites "when of an evil mind we judge amiss of others, for some evil end."[5] His definition has three important components. First, he identifies the *cause* of this sin: "an evil mind." The reason we judge is because we love ourselves and want to appear better than others. Second, he identifies the *manner* of this sin: "we judge amiss of others." We don't deal with people according to the law of charity: "Therefore all things whatsoever ye would that men should do to you, do ye even so to them" (Matt. 7:12). Third, he identifies the *goal* of this sin: "for some evil end." In other words, we don't aim at other people's good—their repentance; on the contrary, we aim at their defamation so that we can make ourselves appear better by comparison. We take consolation (if not satisfaction) from the sins and failures of others because (in some way) it feeds our pride. That's what Christ condemns in this command: "Judge not, that ye be not judged."

Clearly, therefore, there's no contradiction between church discipline and Christ's command. As a matter of fact, it's Christ Himself who implements the practice of church discipline, and in Matthew 18:15–20, He delineates four steps. If the sin is private, the individual is to be admonished privately. If he refuses to listen, he's to be admonished by two or three church members. If he still refuses to listen, he's to be admonished by the whole church. If he still refuses to listen, he's to be cast out of the church.

But what kinds of sin are we talking about? John Owen is very helpful. He makes it clear that church discipline is for those who "continue obstinate in the practice of any *scandalous sin* after private and public admonition."[6] There are three instances of "scandalous sin." The first is *moral*: church discipline is necessary when someone

---

5. Perkins, *Christ's Sermon on the Mount*, 3:195.
6. John Owen, *The True Nature of a Gospel Church*, in *The Works of John Owen*, ed. W. H. Gould (1850; repr., Edinburgh: Banner of Truth, 1977), 16:167 (emphasis in original).

compromises the biblical standards of moral purity (1 Cor. 6:9–11). The second is *doctrinal*: church discipline is necessary when someone rejects the fundamentals of the faith (2 Peter 2:1; 2 John 9–11). The third is *behavioral*: church discipline is necessary when someone disrupts the peace of the church (Rom. 16:17–18; Titus 3:10–11).

In these instances (when the individual continues "obstinate" in his "practice"), we must implement church discipline. Again, according to Owen, such discipline serves three "ends" (or purposes).[7] The first is for the *individual*—"his repentance, reformation, and salvation." The second is for the *world*—the preservation of the church's testimony before unbelievers. The third (and principal) "end" is for the *church*—"its purging and vindication." In other words, church discipline serves to mature believers in the faith. It strengthens the church for evangelism and engagement with the culture. Moreover, it protects the church from decay and corruption.

It is precisely this view of church discipline as a means of grace that has been largely lost. Because of this loss, the church has robbed itself of one of the principal means by which the Holy Spirit cultivates holiness among God's people. The absence of church discipline is tantamount to neglecting the proclamation of the Word (the first mark of the church) or the administration of the sacraments (the second mark of the church). If today's church is to fulfill its calling to convey God's holiness to the world, it must recapture the third mark: the practice of biblical church discipline. And, to a great extent, this responsibility lies with pastors. Do we have "an impartial regard to the fitness of [our] people?"

---

7. Owen, *True Nature of a Gospel Church*, 16:171.

THIRTEEN

A Faithful Shepherd

Like a faithful shepherd, I wish that I might often visit my flock, and warn everyone night and day with tears. May I not expose them—through my absence or negligence—to the rage and cruelty of the devouring wolf. May they never complain of me, "If you had been here, our souls would not have died." Under the law, the priest would visit the homes of lepers to inquire as to their condition. He would give sentence, according to what he discovered. Oh, that I might visit diseased hearts, and diligently inquire how things stand between the great God and their poor souls. May I give them suitable and profitable counsel. On the one hand, I desire a large congregation, because it increases the probability that the gospel will take hold of some. Yet I also desire a small congregation, because it allows me to deal with everyone in private concerning their everlasting peace. Lord, let your strict command frequently come into my mind, "I charge thee therefore before God, and the Lord Jesus Christ, who shall judge the quick and the dead at his appearing and his kingdom: preach the word; be instant in season, out of season; reprove, rebuke, exhort with all long-suffering and doctrine" (2 Tim. 4:1–2).

In 1 Thessalonians 5:14, Paul writes, "Now we exhort you, brethren, warn them that are unruly, comfort the feebleminded, support the weak, be patient toward all men." Here, Paul explains how we're to approach three different groups of people in the context of the

church: the "unruly," "feebleminded," and "weak." One obvious implication of Paul's exhortation is that we actually know our people. How else do we know who to warn, comfort, and support?

Swinnock sees the significance of this. In the above quote, he actually prays for a "small congregation." (Can you imagine anyone praying for such a thing today?) Why? He wants to be able "to deal with everyone in private concerning their everlasting peace." He wants to know his people, so that he can bring God's Word to bear upon their conditions and circumstances. As pastors, do we know our people? Do we know their joys and sorrows, triumphs and defeats? Do we know the "unruly," "feebleminded," and "weak" under our charge? We must (as Swinnock puts it) "diligently inquire how things stand between the great God and their poor souls." How else can we speak God's Word into their lives? How else can we "give them suitable and profitable counsel?"

As we get to know our people, we're called to "preach the word"; to "be instant in season, out of season"; and to "reprove, rebuke, exhort with all long-suffering and doctrine." Here, Paul says five things about our handling of God's Word: it evidences conviction, exposes sin, encourages obedience, exemplifies patience, and emphasizes truth.

First, our handling of God's Word evidences conviction: "Be instant in season, out of season." Peaches have a season, apples have a season, tomatoes have a season, and so on. Paul's point is that preaching is no different. There are fruitful seasons and unfruitful seasons. Either way, we are to be ready, and this readiness stems from our conviction that the Bible is God's Word for God's people. It speaks to every condition and circumstance; it strengthens the weak, comforts the sorrowful, challenges the obstinate, and informs the ignorant.

God's Word is the means by which God's grace comes to His people, and for this reason, it merits our unrivaled devotion. We must remember its "necessity" because, as Swinnock explains, "My soul is sinful, and it is the Word that must sanctify it. My soul is sick, and it is the Word that must heal it. My soul is hungry, and it is the Word that must feed it, or I shall starve. My soul is thirsty, and it is the Word that must satisfy it, or I shall die of thirst." We must also remember the Word's "excellency"; it has "God for its author, Jesus Christ for its matter, and eternal life for its end." Surely, it becomes us "to be serious when the great God is speaking." And we must remember the Word's "efficacy"; God's Word will work one way or the other. "If it works not for your salvation," warns Swinnock, "it will work for your damnation."[1]

Second, our handling of God's Word exposes sin: "reprove, rebuke." These terms mean to correct and admonish, and in reproving and rebuking, we seek to expose sin. As doctors diagnose what ails people physically, pastors diagnose what ails people spiritually because we are physicians of the soul. Sadly, many people want to hear about their perfectibility—not their depravity. They want to hear that God wills their prosperity—not their adversity. They want to hear that God is concerned about their happiness—not their holiness. They want to hear that God is accepting—not that He has ordained a narrow gate that leads to a narrow way. Despite what people want, we must bring God's Word to bear in their lives.

Third, our handling encourages obedience: "exhort." When we exhort, we urge people to respond practically to what they hear from God's Word. The goal of all preaching and teaching is change. When we hear God's Word, we face two choices: we can submit to it, or we can find a church that will tell us what we want to hear. Similarly, when we preach the Word, we face two choices: we can declare it, or we can adapt its teaching to cater to itching ears—the opinions, sentiments, lifestyles, desires, values of the age in which we live.

Fourth, our treatment of God's Word exemplifies patience: "exhort with all long-suffering." Change takes time. The farmer doesn't sow his seed and expect to see a crop the next day; the sun must shine, the rain must fall, the seed must germinate, and the plant must grow. Preaching is no different. It requires great patience, and we must be convinced of this—particularly in light of the prevailing conditions. Today, many people gravitate to preaching that caters to

---

1. Swinnock, *Christian Man's Calling*, 1:150–51.

their passions. The promiscuous want to hear that what they do in private is their own business. The materialists want to hear that their money is for their personal use. The alcoholics want to hear that their sin is a physical disease. The carnal want to hear that they can approach God however they please. The idolaters want to hear that they can serve God while pleasing themselves. The legalists want to hear that God keeps score. The idle want to hear that some sins are mere trifles. The misogynists want to hear that they are exercising their God-given authority in the home. The embittered want to hear that they have a right to be angry. The irresponsible want to hear that someone else is to blame. Oh, the need for long-suffering!

Fifth, our handling of God's Word emphasizes truth: "exhort with…doctrine." A great temptation in preaching is to bypass the mind because it's easier to excite the emotions than edify the mind, to be inspirational rather than instructional. But preaching that bypasses the mind can only engender a temporary response; lasting change is always effected through the mind. We must be renewed in our minds (Rom. 12:1–2), and as we grow in knowledge, the truth embraces the affections, thereby producing change.

This is difficult to sell in today's church. There's growing indifference toward learning in general—doctrine in particular. Some people stop learning once they've finished school; as far as they're concerned, they're done. It's over. They continue to learn by experience, but they cease to learn by studying and never crack open another meaningful book in their lives. Often, that mindset infiltrates the church.

Other people don't like to be challenged. They want to reduce the Christian faith to a few simple statements and sentiments, and they want to hear those same statements and sentiments repeated over and over and over again. They don't want to think outside the box that they've created for themselves. Still other people are far too worldly, and as a result, they're spiritually obtuse. They can't grasp biblical terms and concepts because their minds are too polluted. And so they think the Bible is too dark and difficult or too boring. Or they think doctrine is irrelevant, or theology is pointless. In reality, they're simply too sensual to appreciate those topics. Their lack of appetite for spiritual meat isn't a reflection of the quality of the meat; rather, it's a reflection of their own spiritual immaturity.

Bringing God's Word to bear upon people's lives requires an unwavering conviction concerning the sufficiency of God's Word. Sadly, some people don't appreciate what they have. They're like some of the guests on the *Antiques Roadshow*, who bring an old table or bowl for appraisal only to discover that what they had been using as a workbench or for feeding the dog is worth thousands of dollars. Up until that moment, they had not realized what they had.

When it comes to Scripture, many people are just like that—they don't realize what they have. We must strive to affect our hearts and our people's hearts with its inestimable value. It reveals a glorious God, a great Savior, and a great salvation. It is the means by which God breaks a hard heart, humbles a proud heart, awakens a sleepy heart, enlightens a darkened heart, and regenerates a dead heart. It's the means by which Christ cleanses His bride and the Holy Spirit sanctifies God's people.

Scripture sustains in times of dark affliction, comforts in times of deep sorrow, strengthens in times of danger, guides in times of confusion. It promises the greatest blessings and entitles us to the best inheritance. Scripture has God for its author, Christ for its subject, and eternal life for its end. It's a "special treasure," which God has deposited "into the hands of the children of men."[2]

---

2. Swinnock, *Christian Man's Calling*, 1:141.

FOURTEEN

A Powerful Example

I wish to be like John the Baptist—a burning light in my sermons and a shining light in my actions. May my works never undermine my words. May I never direct others in the right way, while failing to walk in it. Under the law, the priests had the Urim and Thummim, signifying purity of doctrine and sanctity of life. They had a bell and a pomegranate, typifying that preaching and practicing must go together. Oh, that I might preach as powerfully with my life as with my lips. May I avoid those things, although lawful, that will prove a hindrance to others. Nazianzen says that John the Baptist—the voice crying in the wilderness—was all voice, a voice in his habit, a voice in his diet, a voice in his conduct. Lord, enable me to be an example of good works to my people (Titus 2:7). May I be such an example in "word, in conversation, in charity, in spirit, in faith, in purity" (1 Tim. 4:12) that I might be able to say to my flock as Paul to the Philippians, "Brethren, be followers together of me, and mark them which walk so, as ye have us for an ensample" (Phil. 3:17), and as Paul to the Corinthians, "Be ye followers of me, even as I also am of Christ" (1 Cor. 11:1).

Examples are powerful—in both the home and the church. What kind of examples are we? What do people learn from our actions? Our confession is only as compelling as our speech. Our doctrine is only as compelling as our conduct. Our teaching is only as compelling as our love. Our service is only as compelling as our faith. Our activity is only as compelling as our purity. Swinnock gets this. And so, he cries, "Oh, that I might preach as powerfully with my life as with my lips!"

For many pastors, there's a serious disconnect between their private person and public persona. This disconnect is destructive to any church. I believe that's why Paul, when it comes to qualifications for overseers, places so much emphasis on character (1 Tim. 3:1–7; Titus 1:5–9). Interestingly, according to these two texts, Paul only requires that a pastor be able to do two things: teach and manage his family. All of the other requirements are related to character. In a word, a pastor must be "blameless" (1 Tim. 3:2).

When we look at the condition of the church and the connection between "preaching and practicing," perhaps the most pressing need in our day is for pastors to take to heart what it means to be "the husband of one wife" (1 Tim. 3:2). There are numerous schools of thought as to the precise meaning of this statement; however, all agree that a pastor must be faithful to his wife. Are we faithful morally: Have we given our body to her alone? Are we faithful emotionally: Have we given our heart to her alone? Are we faithful spiritually: Do we guide her in godliness? Are we faithful financially: Do we provide for her? Are we faithful physically: Do we protect her? Are we faithful practically: Do we make wise choices?

This call to faithfulness is desperately needed in our day. Our generation (pastors included) has demonstrated a particularly vulnerability to sexual sin. Why? First, it's plagued by a confusion of morals because the present generation has failed to pass its values on to the next. As a result, we're witnessing the rise of a generation with very few moral standards or absolutes. Second, it's plagued by a celebration of vanity. The entertainment industry has just about ruined all that's noble and honorable, and all limitations and boundaries have been crossed. Third, it's plagued by a sense of abandonment. We live in a day scarred by fragmentation. The home has disintegrated, and as a result, most people have a void that they're seeking to fill. Fourth, it's plagued by a loss of shame. All sense of decency is gone.

In such a climate, marital fidelity is under siege. The danger is compounded by the fact that our society often confuses *love* with something else. At times, it's confused with *lust*. Many people equate love with lust. They love chocolate because they enjoy the taste; skiing because they enjoy the rush; cashmere because they enjoy the feel. They love so and so because they enjoy sex. And so love is often restricted to physical attraction and pleasure, and when the novelty of sex wears off, many people assume they aren't in love anymore.

At other times, love is confused with *romance*. It's often depicted as a warm, fuzzy feeling that's beyond our control. And so, we talk about people *falling* in love. They can't help it because the heart has reasons the mind never understands. It's a feeling they must follow. And so, people are constantly falling *in* and *out* of love. After being married for five years, the young man doesn't *feel* the same rush. He reasons to himself: "I guess I'm not in love with her anymore. I'm going to move on. After all, I need to be true to my feelings." He has confused love with some ill-defined concept known as *romance*. Don Carson has his finger on the pulse, when he writes:

> Our society, including many professing Christians, has rejected biblical conceptions of both love and marriage. Love has become a mixture of physical desire and vague sentimentality; marriage has become a provisional sexual union to be terminated when this pathetic, pygmy love dissolves. How different is the biblical perspective. In God's Word, marriage and love are for the tough-minded. Marriage is commitment; and, far from backing out when the going gets rough, marriage partners are to sort out their difficulties in the light of Scripture.[1]

One of the chief reasons marriage exists is pleasure. God designed marriage to delight us—to satisfy us. In the Garden of Eden, God made Eve from one of Adam's ribs then brought Eve to Adam, and the two became one flesh (Gen. 2:21–23). Clearly, God's intention was (and is) that a husband and wife should delight in

---

1. Don Carson, *The Sermon on the Mount: An Evangelical Exposition of Matthew 5–7* (Grand Rapids: Baker, 1978), 46.

each other. This mutual delight is emotional; they enjoy the support, comfort, and encouragement that a God-centered marriage provides. This mutual delight is also physical; they enjoy the conjugal relationship. As an old Puritan once said, "*Due benevolence [i.e., sex]…is one of the most proper and essential acts of marriage… it must be performed with good will and delight, willingly, readily and cheerfully.*"[2] The delight of marriage is really an expression of God's goodness toward us. God is the Creator and God is good; therefore, His creation is good (Gen. 1:31). This necessarily means that marriage is good, and that it's good when a husband and wife delight in each other.

When marriage functions as God intended, it mirrors an even greater reality—the relationship that exists between Christ and His bride. In other words, God has embedded the gospel in the created order by embedding it in marriage. In Ephesians 5:30–31, Paul quotes Genesis 2:23–24, where Moses writes, "And Adam said, This is now bone of my bones, and flesh of my flesh: she shall be called Woman, because she was taken out of Man. Therefore shall a man leave his father and his mother, and shall cleave unto his wife: and they shall be one flesh." In these verses, we discover three important features of the relationship between Adam and Eve. First, Eve is taken out of Adam and, therefore, is flesh of his flesh and bone of his bones. Second, Eve is brought to Adam. They're joined together, in that they cleave to one another, thereby becoming one flesh. Third, Eve completes Adam. Prior to God's creation of Eve, there was no suitable "helper" for Adam (Gen. 2:20). But once God created Eve, Adam was complete.

There are invaluable lessons here concerning the marriage relationship, but that isn't Paul's primary concern. He says, "This is a great mystery: but I speak concerning Christ and the church" (Eph. 5:32). That means the union between Adam and Eve typifies the union between Christ and His church. How? First, as Eve is taken

---

2. William Gouge, *Of Domesticall Duties: Eight Treatises* (London, 1622), 222 (emphasis in original).

out of Adam, so too the church is taken out of Christ. When Christ died, the soldier pierced His side with a spear, and water and blood flowed from that wound: the purchasing price for the church. The church is, therefore, flesh of His flesh and bone of His bones.

Second, as Eve is brought to Adam, so too the church is brought to Christ. They're joined together, becoming one flesh—one body. In the words of Edward Pearse, "Though Christ and the soul were two before, two who were strangers to each other, yet in this marriage or espousal they become one, and so much one that all the world can never make them two again, can never dissolve this union."[3]

Third, as Eve completes Adam, so too the church completes Christ. As the eternal Son of God, Christ is perfect and complete. However, as Mediator, He's incomplete without His people. As Paul declares, the church is "his body, the fullness of him that filleth all in all" (Eph. 1:23).

An appreciation of how the relationship between husband and wife mirrors the relationship between Christ and His church liberates marriage from its modern-day caricature as a trap, chore, or burden. It frees marriage from the selfish, self-centered, self-serving, self-gratifying convenience or inconvenience that it has become. It elevates marriage into the realm of the divine and sets it apart as one of the most sacred callings the world has ever known.

With this view of marriage before us, we must seek to be "the husband of one wife." We must also cultivate poverty of spirit, cling to God in prayer, feed on God's Word, control our thought life, and guard our eyes and hearts. We must keep busy in God's work, avoid undue familiarities, and bring "into captivity every thought to the obedience of Christ" (2 Cor. 10:5). Above all these, we must be faithful to our wives, remembering that the greatest sermon we ever preach is our marriage.

---

3. Edward Pearse, *The Best Match; or, The Soul's Espousal to Christ* (Morgan, Pa.: Soli Deo Gloria, 1994), 6–7.

FIFTEEN

A Humble Instrument

When my labor is unfruitful, I wish that I might not be discouraged, knowing that I am "unto God a sweet savor of Christ, in them that who are saved, and in them that are perishing" (2 Cor. 2:15). "Though Israel be not gathered, yet shall I be glorious in the eyes of the LORD. And my God shall be my strength" (Isa. 49:5). Oh, that I might not be sent to make their hearts dull, ears heavy, and eyes blind, "lest they see with their eyes, and hear with their ears, and understand with their heart, and convert, and be healed" (Isa. 6:10). Rather, may I turn many sinners from error, save many souls from death, and hide a multitude of sins. When Joab took the city of Rabbah, he was willing to have the crown set on the king's head (2 Sam. 12:27). Likewise, when my God enables me to cast down high things that exalt themselves against the knowledge of Him, and bring many sinners into captivity to the obedience of Christ, I wish that I might set the crown of glory upon God's head alone. I am a mere instrument; He is the principal efficient. I am a mere pipe; He is the spring from which the water of life flows. I merely apply the remedy; He bestows the healing. Oh, that I might never be so ungrateful as to dishonor Him by thinking of myself above what is proper. May all my services magnify His name and glorify His praise.

Pastoral ministry is fraught with challenges. Here, Swinnock addresses two of the most common: unfruitfulness and fruitfulness. Simply put, no matter what happens in ministry—fruit or no fruit, growth or no growth—we'll face one of these two challenges. Why? As Swinnock explains, unfruitfulness leads to discouragement, while fruitfulness leads to pride.

As for the *challenge of unfruitfulness,* Swinnock prays, "When my labor is unfruitful, I wish that I might not be discouraged." It's easy to preach when people flock to hear. It's easy to counsel when relationships are healed. It's easy to evangelize when people are sincerely seeking. It's easy to lead when people are eager to follow. It's easy to teach when people are attentive and appreciative. But what happens when the opposite is true, when our efforts are fruitless? How do we keep going in the day of small things or when opposition is daunting? What do we do when the church is carnal and superficial or we're worn out—physically, emotionally, and spiritually? To sum up, what happens when ministry seems pointless? In Greek mythology, Zeus punishes King Sisyphus (in the underworld) by making him roll a boulder up a hill without ever reaching the top. Whenever he nears the top, the boulder rolls back down; Sisyphus is powerless to stop it, and he must start again. Frustrating activities are sometimes described as *Sisyphean.* I know pastors who view their ministry as *Sisyphean*—pointless.

This feeling of discouragement is compounded by the fact that many of us tend to idealize the past. Certainly, we should learn from the past; as the adage goes, "whoever neglects the past is destined to repeat it." But we must also understand that every age has its highlights and lowlights, strengths and weaknesses, and we must refrain from making too much of the past. Are we paralyzed in the present because we're living in the past? Are we discouraging others in the present because we're enamored with a romanticized concept of the past? "Say not thou, What is the cause that the former days were better than these? For thou dost not inquire wisely concerning this" (Eccl. 7:10).

What is Swinnock's remedy for the discouragement that arises during seasons of unfruitfulness? It's very simple—he delights in the fact he's "unto God a sweet savor of Christ." In other words,

Swinnock doesn't derive his identity from his ministry, but from Christ. He doesn't derive his sense of self-worth from his ministry, but from Christ. In short, he doesn't make an idol of his ministry.

Am I discouraged? If so, it's time to look at Christ. John Owen declares, "Let us live in constant contemplation of Christ's glory. As we do, virtue will proceed from Him to repair our spiritual decay, to renew a right spirit within us, and to cause us to abound in obedience.... When our souls are filled with thoughts of Christ and His glory, they will discard all causes of spiritual weakness.... Nothing will so much excite and encourage our souls as a constant view of Christ and His glory."[1]

As for the *challenge of fruitfulness*, Swinnock prays, "When my God enables me to cast down high things that exalt themselves against the knowledge of Him, and bring many sinners into captivity to the obedience of Christ, I wish that I might set the crown of glory upon God's head alone." Here, Swinnock acknowledges his susceptibility and vulnerability to pride. When people speak well of us, when pews are full, when building projects are in the works, we're in very dangerous territory indeed. These things will feed our pride.

The disciples ask Christ: "Who is the greatest in the kingdom of heaven?" (Matt. 18:1). We don't know what precipitates their question, but we do know what's at the root of it—pride. Christ responds by placing a child in their midst and declaring, "Verily I say unto you, Except ye be converted, and become as little children, ye shall not enter into the kingdom of heaven" (v. 3). What does He mean? To answer that question, we must be careful to distinguish between being *childish* and *childlike*. To be *childish* is to be immature. The Bible warns us not to be *childish* in the way we think or behave (Matt. 11:16; 1 Cor. 14:20; Eph. 4:14). Therefore, when Christ says we must "become as little children," He most certainly isn't saying we should be *childish*. He's affirming that we should be *childlike*.

---

1. John Owen, *Meditations and Discourses Concerning the Glory of Christ*, in *The Works of John Owen,* ed. W. H. Gould (1850; repr., Edinburgh: Banner of Truth, 1977), 1:460–61.

How? He tells us: "Whosoever therefore shall humble himself as this little child, the same is the greatest in the kingdom of heaven" (Matt. 18:4). Here, Christ calls His disciples' attention to the fact that children are completely dependent upon adults for survival. By extension, He's telling them that they must rid themselves of any desire for greatness, and admit their child-like dependence upon God for all things. That is to say, they must humble themselves.

Humility, according to Jonathan Edwards, is "a habit of mind and heart corresponding to our comparative unworthiness and vileness before God, or a sense of our own comparative meanness in His sight, with the disposition to a behavior answerable thereto."[2] Here, Edwards mentions two kinds of humility.[3] First, he speaks of *natural* humility, which arises from a perception of our "meanness" (or smallness) as creatures before God. In other words, it arises when we compare ourselves to God's *natural* excellence (i.e., His greatness). We're weak in comparison to His power, foolish in comparison to His wisdom, ignorant in comparison to His knowledge, and small in comparison to His sovereignty.

Second, Edwards speaks of *moral* humility, which arises from a perception of our "vileness" as sinners before God. In other words, it arises when we compare ourselves to God's *moral* excellence (i.e., His goodness). We recognize that we've sinned against God's grace and mercy and, that we're therefore without moral virtues adequate to commend ourselves to God. As a result, we're aware of our utter dependence upon Him.

In a word, humility arises from a biblical understanding of who we are and who God is. And it leads to absolute submission to God and absolute dependence upon Him. In seasons of fruitfulness, we must be mindful of our susceptibility to pride. These are times (unlike any other) when we must "become as little children." Such humility must shape *why* we minister—God's grace is the principle from which our ministry flows—and it must shape *how* we

---

2. Edwards, *Charity and Its Fruits*, 130.
3. Edwards, *Charity and Its Fruits*, 133–34.

minister—God's glory is the objective at which our ministry aims. The greater God becomes in our eyes, the smaller we become in our own eyes. And our chief desire is (as Swinnock prays) that all our service might "magnify His name and glorify His praise."

SIXTEEN

A Watchful Overseer

Finally, I wish that I might take heed to myself, my doctrine, and my life. May I be watchful in all things, endure affliction, prove my ministry, do the work of a faithful pastor, lest—like they who prophesied and cast out demons in Christ's name—I be cast to demons as a worker of iniquity, and find the gate of life, which I opened to others, shut against me (Matt. 7:21–23; 1 Tim. 4:16; 2 Tim. 4:5). Oh, let me not—as porters in great houses—lodge outside while I let others into heaven! Let it please Thee, O God of all grace, to fill me with the fruit of Thy Spirit that I might feed Thy people with knowledge and understanding, "taking the oversight thereof, not by constraint, but willingly; not for filthy lucre, but of a ready mind; neither as being [a lord] over God's heritage, but being [an ensample] to the flock. And when the chief Shepherd shall appear [I] shall receive a crown of glory that fadeth not away" (1 Peter 5:2–4).

Swinnock wants to avoid anything that will compromise his ministry. With this concern before him, he asks God to help him "take heed" to himself. When I was in college, I worked during the summer months for a roofing company; it was hard work and also a little dangerous, at times. There wasn't anything particularly dangerous about working on a one-story home, but occasionally, we worked on taller buildings, and whenever we did, I watched my every step. Why? I understood the consequences of one misstep. That's

Swinnock's point. As pastors, one misstep can be disastrous. For this reason, we should be "watchful in all things."

According to John Flavel, watchfulness consists of six "acts."[1] First, we examine the "frame" of our hearts in the light of Scripture. Second, we cultivate "deep humiliation" on account of the evil in our hearts. Third, we pray earnestly for "heart-purifying" and "heart-rectifying" grace. Fourth, we discipline ourselves to walk with God, avoiding all occasions to sin. Fifth, we develop a "holy jealousy" over our hearts. Sixth, we live in the realization of God's presence.

Of these six "acts," the first is perhaps most fundamental: we examine the "frame" of our hearts in the light of Scripture. For Swinnock, such self-examination involves "serious consideration… an act of the practical understanding, whereby it reflects upon its actions and intentions, and comparing them with the rule of the Word, proceeds to lay its command upon the will and affections to put what is good in execution."[2] To do this, Swinnock encourages the use of *soliloquies,* whereby we "confer" and "commune" with our hearts.[3] He remarks:

> If you want to walk closely with God, and keep even with Him, reckon daily with Him, and call yourself to a strict scrutiny. What am I doing? How am I living? Is my life the life of faith and holiness? Am I in God's way and under His protection? Do I have the truth of grace and the power of godliness, or do I please myself with the form of it? Do I thrive and increase in grace, or do I decay and decline? Suppose I were to die this night, what ground do I have to hope for heaven, what assurance that I will escape the power and rage of frightful devils, what evidence that I am a new creature, engrafted into Christ, and thereby entitled to life and blessedness? Thus feel

---

1. John Flavel, *Saint Indeed: or, The Great Work of a Christian, Opened and Pressed,* in *The Works of John Flavel* (1820; repr., London: Banner of Truth, 1968), 5:426–28. As Flavel makes clear, these six "acts" are the duty of all believers.

2. Swinnock, *Door of Salvation Opened,* 5:123.

3. Swinnock, *Christian Man's Calling,* 2:451.

the pulse of your soul, inquire into its state, visit it often, and see how it does.[4]

From the above, it's evident that *soliloquies* consist of a series of questions and answers, designed to make us "feel the pulse" of our hearts for the purpose of self-evaluation.[5] As pastors, we must ask ourselves the hard questions. What's the *principle* of my life? In other words, why do I do what I do? What do I love and hate? What do I want, desire, and crave? What do I think about? What shapes my dreams, choices, ambitions, and priorities? Is my chief desire to please myself, please others, or please God? What's the *pattern* of my life? Who do I esteem and emulate? Who do I want to be like? Why? What do I want for my wife and children? What do I think will make them truly happy? Where do I turn in times of trial and affliction? Where do I find help, solace, refuge, escape, and security? What's the *purpose* of my life? What occupies my time? Have I dedicated everything to God, yet wish that I had more to give? Our answers to these questions reveal the condition of our heart.

The motivation for such watchfulness comes from the realization that we live and serve in God's presence. In his first letter to Timothy, Paul writes, "I give thee charge in the sight of God, who quickeneth all things, and before Christ Jesus, who before Pontius Pilate witnessed a good confession" (1 Tim. 6:13). In his second letter, he adds, "I charge thee therefore before God, and the Lord Jesus Christ, who shall judge the quick and the dead at his appearing and his kingdom" (2 Tim. 4:1). As Paul delivers these charges to Timothy, he reminds him of the simple fact that he ministers in God's sight. Why does he do that? He wants this realization to have a sobering effect upon Timothy. It should have a sobering effect upon us. As pastors, we must develop the mindset that our lives are open to God's continual gaze.

---

4. Swinnock, *Christian Man's Calling*, 3:144.

5. Richard Baxter describes soliloquies as "awakening questions." *The Practical Works of Richard Baxter: Select Treatises* (1863; repr., Grand Rapids: Baker, 1981), 548.

Regrettably, many of us believe God sees, yet that belief makes little difference in the way we live. In 2011, the Boston Bruins beat the Vancouver Canucks in the Stanley Cup Finals, and an orgy of destruction erupted in downtown Vancouver after the final game. Traffic cameras mounted at intersections and security cameras mounted on stores and offices captured the destruction, while hundreds of people with cell-phone cameras recorded the faces of those responsible. It took the police thousands of hours to watch all the video footage. Here's my point: the rioters knew about the cameras, but it didn't stop them from engaging in wanton destruction. Similarly, many of us know God sees, but it doesn't affect the way we live.

We must grasp the fact that living in God's presence involves much more than simply acknowledging He sees. To live in God's presence is to possess a deep sense of His *majesty* and *mercy*. Because of His love, the Son of God veiled His majesty. He left a glorious crown, walked in our flesh, and took our infirmities. He gave sight to the blind, speech to the mute, hearing to the deaf, and life to the dead. He was hungry, thirsty, and weary. He was sorrowful unto death. He was betrayed, arrested, and condemned. He was crowned with thorns, scourged with whips, and pierced with nails. He hung on a shameful cross, bearing our guilt and shame. He "poured out his soul unto death" (Isa. 53:12). He was punished, so that we might be pardoned. He was wounded, so that we might be healed. He was condemned, so that we might be justified. That's *majesty* and *mercy*—the gospel. When the Holy Spirit impresses this upon our hearts, the result is transformative. We live in God's presence, meaning we fear to offend Him and long to please Him. And that's the fountain from which watchfulness flows.

PART 2

Part 1 highlighted what Swinnock calls "the properties and duties of a conscientious pastor." A recurring emphasis in this list is the importance of labor and love to pastoral ministry. According to Swinnock, these two are "chiefly requisite in a pastor." As the soul and body are the essential parts of a man, labor and love are "the whole of a minister." Because of this conviction, Swinnock turns his attention to explaining the essential relationship between labor and love in his sermon "The Pastor's Farewell." He preached this sermon upon his departure from his church in Rickmansworth, where he had ministered for eleven years. The following is an edited version.

The Pastor's Farewell

And now brethren, I commend you to God, and to the word of his grace, which is able to build you up, and to give you an inheritance among all them which are sanctified.
—Acts 20:32

Books on human history are of such value that authors usually dedicate them to honored individuals as worthy of their serious perusal. Surely then, books on divine history (such as the Acts of the Apostles, which contains the heroic acts of Christ's servants in their combat with and conquest over—not only men and the world—but sin and the devil) deserve the attention of noble Theophilus (Acts 1:1), of great and small, and of all people.

Introduction

The four Gospels contain the great mystery of Christ—the Head of the church. The Acts of the Apostles contains the glorious history of the church—the body of Christ. The first part of the book (chapters 1–13) deals with all the apostles. The second part (chapter 14–28) deals with Paul's travels and trials—as his conversion is most miraculous, so his ministry is most illustrious. In chapter 20, we find him on his fourth journey, arriving at Miletus—a city on the border of Ionia and Caesarea, close to the Aegean Sea. He sends for the elders of the Ephesian church. His message to them consists of four parts.

1. Paul's Vindication of His Ministry

Pastors must watch—not only their consciences—but their reputations. When a pastor's name is contemptible, his doctrine is less acceptable. That is the reason why the apostle defends himself.

First, the apostle defends the integrity of his life: "Ye know, from the first that I came into Asia, after what manner I have been with you at all seasons, serving the Lord with all humility of mind, and with many tears, and temptations, which befell me by the lying in wait of the Jews" (Acts 20:18–19). It is excellent when a pastor can appeal to his people's consciences as evidence of the purity of his conduct. Holy pastors are "angels" (Rev. 2:1, 8, 12, 18), but unholy pastors degenerate into devils: "Have I not chosen you twelve, and one of you is a devil?" (John 6:70).

Second, the apostle defends the fidelity of his doctrine: "Ye know…how I kept back nothing that was profitable unto you, but have shewed you, and have taught you publicly, and from house to house" (Acts 20:20). The steward, who distributes a proper portion to everyone under his charge, is faithful. Similarly, pastors declare their love for their people through their holy conduct and faithful labor. They teach with their lips and confirm their teaching with their lives. In so doing, they are like stars, directing their people.

2. Paul's Exhortation to the Elders

As he taught them with his example, so the apostle teaches them with his commands: "Take heed therefore unto yourselves, and to all the flock, over the which the Holy Ghost hath made you overseers" (Acts 20:28). That is to say, these elders must devote their care and study to their and their people's welfare. Like good shepherds, they must work and watch night and day for the good of their sheep. The apostle urges this counsel for three reasons.

First, he appeals to the person who appointed the elders: "the Holy Ghost hath made you overseers" (v. 28). They must be faithful, because the Holy Spirit has called them. Unfaithfulness is a felony when it is against a subject, but it is treason when it is against a sovereign. It is a trifling with the Most High God's trust.

Second, he appeals to the price paid for the church: "to feed the church of God, which he hath purchased with his own blood" (v. 28). Things of great cost require great care. Souls are infinitely precious and, therefore, deserve our utmost effort. If God considers His people worthy of His blood, we should esteem them worthy of our sweat.

Third, he appeals to the peril facing the church: "For I know this, that after my departing shall grievous wolves enter in among you, not sparing the flock. Also of your own selves shall men arise, speaking perverse things, to draw away disciples after them. Therefore watch" (vv. 29–31). If wolves watch to devour the sheep, then shepherds must watch to defend the sheep. When an attack on the garrison is certain, commanders must always be on guard.

3. Paul's Prediction of His Future Suffering
"And now, behold, I go bound in the spirit to Jerusalem, not knowing the things that shall befall me there: save that the Holy Ghost witnesseth in every city, saying that bonds and afflictions abide me" (Acts 20:22–23). Of all people, Christians must bear their crosses. Of all Christians, pastors must expect to undergo misery. The more good a pastor possesses, the more evil he must expect.

"And now, behold, I know that ye all, among whom I have gone preaching the kingdom of God, shall see my face no more" (v. 25). This is sad news for two reasons. First, the church needs the apostle. He has warned them of the danger of wolves entering among them. Now, they will be without their guide—like sailors without their captain in the midst of the storm, or like soldiers without their commander in the midst of the battle. The realization that their nanny will be taken from them, before they are able to walk on their own, afflicts their hearts. Second, the church loves the apostle. In all likelihood, he was their spiritual parent, who had birthed them, raised them, and assisted them in every condition. Therefore, they lament their loss of him.

4. Paul's Commendation of the Elders to God
"And now brethren, I commend you to God, and to the word of his grace, which is able to build you up, and to give you an inheritance

among all them which are sanctified" (Acts 20:32). Having given them a command from God, the apostle now commends them to God. His words contain the legacy he leaves to his Christian friends. He bids farewell, and prays for their welfare.

(1) "And now"
The apostle is their guide, but he must soon depart. He foresees that fierce wolves will seek their ruin. What else can he do but commend them to God, who can protect them? This is the greatest kindness he can do. Like a dying father, he commits them—his children—to a faithful guardian. He must leave them. He will never see them again. But he entrusts them to God, who will never leave them nor forsake them.

(2) "Brethren"
This term speaks of the apostle's humility. These men are his inferiors, yet he refers to them as equals. Brothers stand on the same level. This term also speaks of the apostle's affection: "love as brethren" (1 Peter 3:8). It points to how near and dear these men are to him. Like water, love does not easily run upward, but it does run swiftly and pleasantly on level ground. The apostle loves them and esteems them as brothers. Providence is separating them, but he demonstrates his deep affection for them by committing them to God, from whom no one can separate them.

(3) "I commend you to God"
In our day, we commend others by praising them for some worth in them. The term is used in that sense in Scripture: "I commend unto you Phoebe our sister" (Rom. 16:1). However, in our text, to commend means to commit to the tender custody of the blessed God. The apostle does not want them to be discouraged by his departure. He commits them to God, who will abundantly make up for his absence by His almighty power and favorable presence. Although the apostle is leaving them, he commends them to God, who will care for them and never fail them. God has infinite strength for their protection, infinite wisdom for their direction, and infinite favor for their consolation.

(4) "And to the word of his grace"

The Scripture is God's Word because, as people reveal their wills in their words, so God manifests His mind and pleasure in the Scripture. The expression "the word of his grace" refers to that part of Scripture which speaks of God's good will and pleasure toward people (Acts 20:24; Titus 2:11). Because of their sin and rebellion, people cannot attain happiness by their own works. But God is pleased to accept Christ's perfect obedience on behalf of believing Christians. This act of infinite grace, as revealed in the gospel, is most fitly called "the word of his grace." The law speaks fury and death, but the gospel speaks favor and life. The law wounds with its blows, but the gospel heals with its ointment. The law condemns without pity to the sufferings of hell, but the gospel saves by mercy from the wrath to come.

Now, the apostle commends his fainting patients to this rich medicine: "the word of his grace." It would be little comfort to be commended to a righteous and jealous God—as grass committed to a consuming fire. For this reason, he tells them: "I commend you to God"—not an angry Judge, but a gracious Father and compassionate Friend. If they doubt it, they must look at the gospel, in which they will see God's eternal plan to magnify His grace in them. The apostle commends them to that word of God's grace, in which every line speaks of His love and every expression speaks of His tender affection. The apostle knows their poverty, but the word of God's grace is a mine of unsearchable riches. They are hungry, but it is bread. They are weary, but it is rest. Whatever their condition, it provides suitable comfort.

(5) "Which is able to build you up"

According to some scholars, these words refer to "the word of his grace." According to others, they refer to God. The uncertainty exists because both terms are in the same gender. It is, therefore, difficult to determine the antecedent. Either way, both are true: God is able to build them up, and the gospel (or "the word of his grace") is able to build them up. God is the first cause and principal efficient, whereas "the word of his grace" is the second cause and subordinate instrument. The gospel cannot do it without God, and God will not do it without the gospel. By the gospel, God saves, sanctifies, edifies, and gives an inheritance.

The apostle's point is that the foundation of godliness is already laid in their hearts, but something is still lacking—a greater degree of grace and holiness. He knows that his brothers are not content with a bare knowledge of Christ. They desire to grow in the grace and knowledge of Christ. That is why they grieve over their loss of him. As a faithful steward, he had furthered the welfare of their souls by giving them their spiritual food in due season. Now they fear they will starve without him. And so he commends them to the same master (God) and food ("the word of his grace") by which they had already grown. These are still able to communicate the same strength.

(6) "And to give you an inheritance"
God's children desire two things—proficiency in grace and perfection in glory. The apostle commends these elders to God (and "the word of his grace"), who alone can satisfy both desires: progress in holiness and possession of happiness. The saints are heirs, joint heirs with Christ (Rom. 8:17). Heaven is their proper and peculiar inheritance: "the inheritance of the saints in light" (Col. 1:12). The gospel (or "the word of his grace") purifies and prepares them for it. It is also the deed, which conveys their right and title to it. That is why it is called the gospel of our salvation. God is the author and donor of it. Glory is His free gift: "it is your Father's good pleasure to give you the kingdom" (Luke 12:32).

(7) "Among all them which are sanctified"
All the inhabitants of heaven are holy. Those who are glorified must first be sanctified. The temple's inner court is a type of heaven. Only the priests, who were holy to God, could enter. Saints are priests—a holy priesthood (Rev. 1:6).

Summary
The sum of the whole verse is as follows. Infinitely wise providence sees fit to deprive the Ephesian church of the apostle's presence. He

knows they desire a further degree of sanctification and its final consummation. Therefore, he commits and commends them to God. By God's strength, "the word of his grace" is able to give them growth in grace while they live and the crown of glory when they die—among all those who are partakers of the same hope and holiness.

Observations

The verse consists of three parts. First, there is the compellation: "brethren." The saints are a society of brothers: "Love the brotherhood" (1 Peter 2:17). In contrast, the company of sinners is a rabble of conspirators. Second, there is the commendation: "And now brethren, I commend you." This commendation is amplified by its object: he commends them to God as the fountain of their grace and happiness, and to the gospel (or "the word of his grace") as the channel which conveys these things to them. This commendation is also amplified by its effect: its proficiency—"which is able to build you up," and perfection—"which is able to…give you an inheritance among all them which are sanctified." Third, there is the occasion: "And now." Without a doubt, the apostle had commended them to God on many occasions—he remembered them in his prayers without ceasing (Eph. 1:16). But now, as he leaves them, he commends them in a special manner to God's care.

I will draw some observations from the verse, and then affirm the doctrine which I intend to develop.

1. Godliness Is No Enemy to Courtesy

The apostle is ready to depart. He does not leave abruptly, but solemnly: "And now brethren." Some Christians erroneously assume that good works and good manners are inconsistent. Although Christianity removes the pretentious expressions of courtesy, it does not destroy courtesy. Civil language and courteous behavior are not essential to Christianity, but they do adorn it. God's saints are always courteous. The apostle spends the greatest part of this chapter in courteous greetings. He would not have done so if it had been unlawful or unnecessary.

2. *Grace Turns Civil Courtesy into Serious Christianity*

The apostle does not bid them a mere civil farewell, according to human custom. Rather, he solemnly bids farewell by commending them to the blessed God: "And now brethren, I commend you to God." The ungodly debase sacred actions, while the godly advance civil actions. Grace gives a savor to all our actions, thereby making them healthier to our souls. It even sanctifies our greetings: "Salute one another with an holy kiss" (Rom. 16:16). Kissing is a civil action, which becomes sacred among the godly—"an holy kiss."

3. *Christians Are Brothers*

The saints are united in the bond of brotherhood: "And now brethren." It was customary for early Christians to call those of the same communion "brothers" and "sisters." They are brothers, in that they have the same Father: "And I will be a Father unto you, and ye shall be my sons and daughters, saith the Lord Almighty" (2 Cor. 6:18). God both adopts and regenerates them (John 1:12; James 1:21). They are brothers, in that they have the same mother: "But Jerusalem which is above is free, which is the mother of us all" (Gal. 4:26). They wear the same clothing, dine at the same table, and dwell in the same house. They are united under the same head, renewed with the same heart, and travel to the same heaven.

Furthermore, the saints are brothers in regard of affection. The curtains of the tabernacle were joined together with loops, and so are true Christians with love. They love as brothers, and seek one another's good and welfare. Their gifts are not for their private profit, but for the advantage of others. Their desires are not confined to their own dwellings. In their prayers, they reach thousands whom they could never meet on earth: "For my brethren and companions' sakes, I will now say, Peace be within thee" (Ps. 122:8). They sympathize with one another's suffering and rejoice in one another's solace. Every saint is a great merchant who has investors all over the world trading for him at the throne of grace.

4. The Gospel Is the Word of God's Grace

In Scripture, the word "grace" refers to favor (or goodwill) and its effect (or fruit). In both respects, the gospel is fitly called "the word of his grace." Why? First, the gospel contains God's infinite grace toward sinners. The law speaks of humanity's bottomless misery, but the gospel speaks of God's boundless mercy. The law is a court of justice, but the gospel is a throne of grace. Grace sits as a commander-in-chief in the gospel. As Ahasuerus to Esther, it holds out the golden scepter of mercy to condemned sinners, so that they can touch it with the hand of faith (Esther 5:2). The sum of the gospel is expressed in the song of the angelic choir: "Glory to God in the highest, and on earth peace, good will toward men" (Luke 2:14). The substance of God's love was never revealed until the preaching of the gospel. Before then, it ran like an underground river. In the gospel, it burst forth, showing itself. Now, it refreshes us with its pleasant streams. The law is a warrant for our arrest and execution, but the gospel is a full pardon. Choosing grace (Eph. 1:5), calling grace (2 Tim. 1:9), justifying grace (Rom. 3:24), and glorifying grace (1 Peter 3:7) are all revealed in the gospel. Therefore, it is appropriately called "the word of his grace."

Second, the gospel is the effect (or fruit) of God's grace toward sinners. Some people observe that dew never falls in stormy weather. The same is true of God's grace. The dew of the gospel falling on a scorched heart is a sign of a calm and serene heaven. This rain of the gospel softens and cleanses. The fact that our part of the world is wet with this dew, while other parts are dry, is merely from grace: "I caused it to rain upon one city, and caused it not to rain upon another city" (Amos 4:7).

Third, the gospel is the means of conversion. As manna fell with the dew around the Israelites' tents (Ex. 16:4), so grace falls with the gospel. Many of the Israelites heard the thundering of Sinai and the threatening of the law without being moved. But the apostle wins their children with the promises of the gospel: "Received ye the Spirit by the works of the law, or by the hearing of faith?" (Gal. 3:2). The ice is hardened with the cold and melted with the sun. When the murderers of our Savior heard the gospel, they were pricked to the heart (Acts 2:37).

5. *The Gospel Is Effectual for Conversion and Edification*
The word of God's grace "is able to build you up." It brings forth souls to Christ, and builds up souls in Christ. Christians are born by the gospel: "in Christ Jesus I have begotten you through the gospel" (1 Cor. 4:15). They also grow by the gospel: "As newborn babes, desire the sincere milk of the word, that ye may grow thereby" (1 Peter 2:2).

6. *The Gospel Carries Christians to Glory*
The word of God's grace "is able…to give you an inheritance." Like Moses, it leads the saints out of Egypt, delivers them from bondage to their lusts, and conducts them through the wilderness of the world. And, like Joshua, it brings the saints into Canaan—the land of promise. It is called "the grace of God," which brings salvation (Titus 2:11). It brings salvation to people and people to salvation.

7. *Heaven Is an Inheritance*
An inheritance is an estate that a father leaves to his son. The saints are God's first-born sons and, therefore, heirs. God's natural Son is His natural heir, but His adopted sons are His adopted heirs. Therefore, they receive an inheritance from their Father. People receive their inheritance by virtue of natural birth, but saints receive their inheritance by virtue of spiritual birth. Their inheritance is incomparable. Earthly possessions are nothing in comparison to it. Their right to it is unalterable, for it is an inheritance "reserved in heaven" (1 Peter 1:4). It can never be taken from them, for it is in God's keeping.

8. *The Inheritance Belongs to Those Who Are Holy*
Only the children of God, who are born again, are heirs of this inheritance: "Among all them which are sanctified." Heaven is undefiled and, therefore, all the inhabitants of heaven must be sanctified. If a carnal, unsanctified person were to enter heaven, he would make

God a liar: "And there shall in no wise enter into it anything that defileth" (Rev. 21:27). In heaven, the saints enter into God's immediate service. Will the great King be served by unclean vessels?

Exposition

The doctrine that I intend to develop is this: The greatest good a pastor can do for his people—whom he must leave—is to commend them to God. "And now brethren, I commend you to God, and to the word of his grace." The apostle has a great love and tender respect for his brothers. How does he manifest it? He commends them to God. It is the greatest kindness for Christians to commit their friends to God. When parents leave their children, they commit them to a faithful caregiver. When Paul and Barnabas arrived at Derbe, they commended the brothers to God (Acts 14:23). Before Jacob died, he commended his sons to the living God (Gen. 48:15–16, 49). Before Moses departed, he commended the Israelites to God's protection (Deut. 22, 23).

Our blessed Savior, who provides an unparalleled pattern and precedent, does not leave His disciples fatherless when He departs from the world and returns to the Father. He knows His disciples' hearts are heavy. For this reason, He commends them to God. This is the greatest good, which His boundless love can do for them. "And now I am no more in the world, but these are in the world, and I come to thee. Holy Father, keep through thine own name those whom thou hast given me.... I pray not that thou shouldest take them out of the world, but that thou shouldest keep them from the evil" (John 17:11, 15). Christ affectionately entreats His Father to take care of them. He uses multiple arguments to prevail with His Father to be the guide and guardian of His children. "Father, I must leave them. Love and keep them, so that they may not be left alone. Father, I do not ask for their immediate translation to glory, but their preservation in a state of grace. I do not desire that they should be kept from the evil of affliction, but from the evil in affliction. The world hates them for Thy sake. What will become of them, if Thou dost not help them?"

In the exposition of the text, I will show how a pastor is to commend his people to God, and why it is the greatest good he can do for them.

1. How a Pastor Commends His People to God
This is done in two ways.

(1) A pastor commends his people to God through prayer
The departing parent appoints his executor to be careful of, and faithful to, his children. In so doing, he commends them to him. Likewise, a departing pastor entreats God to be gracious to, and mindful of, his people. By preaching, a pastor commends God to his people's acceptance. By prayer, he commends his people to God's blessing. Under the law, the principal part of the priest's office was to pray and offer sacrifice for the people. Aaron had to bear the names of the children of Israel before God. In a similar fashion, a pastor's main work is to stand between God and his people by giving commands from God to them and by offering prayers to God for them: "On this wise ye shall bless the children of Israel, saying unto them, 'the LORD bless thee, and keep thee'" (Num. 6:23–24). A pastor blesses his people when he asks God to bless them. God blesses His people by commanding a blessing on them: "For there the LORD commanded the blessing, even life for evermore" (Ps. 133:3). God's blessing is operative, whereas a pastor's blessing is optative. A pastor wishes the blessing, but God works the blessing.

The apostle makes prayer the alpha and omega, the beginning and ending, of his epistles. If we look carefully, we will find that each of them is scented with this sweet perfume (Rom. 1:9; 15:13; 16:24; 1 Cor. 1:3–4; 16:23; 2 Cor. 1:2–3; 13:14; Gal. 1:3; 6:18; Eph. 1:2–3, 15–20; 6:23–24; Phil. 1:2–4, 9–11; 4:23; Col. 1:2–3; 4:18; 1 Thess. 1:2; 3:10; 5:28; 2 Thess. 1:2; 2:16; 3:18; 1 Tim. 1:2; 6:21; 2 Tim. 1:2; 4:22; Titus 1:4; 3:15; Philemon 4). Prayer is his salutation and conclusion. Some people seal their letters with their signature. The apostle seals his epistles with prayer: "The salutation of Paul with mine own hand, which is the token in every epistle: so I write. The grace of our Lord Jesus Christ be with you all. Amen" (2 Thess. 3:17–18). All

Christians must pray for others. It is their general calling. But it is a pastor's particular calling. He must give himself to prayer. It must be the element in which he breathes and lives: "He is a prophet, and he shall pray for thee" (Gen. 20:7). Of all men, prophets must be frequent in prayer.

There are some people whom pastors must, in a special manner, commend to God in their prayers—namely, those whom God has committed to their special charge. A good housekeeper will help his neighbors and strangers, but he has greater regard for those of his family. Like Sir Francis Drake's ship, our prayers must encompass the whole world: "I exhort therefore, that, first of all, supplications, prayers, intercessions, and giving of thanks, be made for all men" (1 Tim. 2:1). The higher a man is, the farther he sees. The richer a man is, the more he assists. The higher a man is in holiness, the farther he sees into others' needs. The richer a man is in grace, the more he prays for the relief of others' needs. But, in the wide earth, a pastor's eye must principally be on God's vineyard, to water it with his tears, and to request heaven's influence for the refreshing and ripening of its fruit: "Praying always, with all prayer and supplication in the Spirit…for all saints" (Eph. 6:18). Christ teaches this in the prayer of prayers: "Our Father" (Matt. 6:9). The term "Father" speaks of faith in God. The term "our" speaks of brotherly love. In this vineyard, a pastor's love and labor must focus on that part which is committed to his trust. Prayer is a debt owed to all people: Samuel declares, "Moreover as for me, God forbid that I should sin against the LORD in ceasing to pray for you" (1 Sam. 12:23). But prayer is a special obligation owed to a pastor's church: "We are bound to thank God always for you" (2 Thess. 1:3). A pastor's prayers are the common property of the church, in which everyone has a share. He must be sure to remember his own people at the throne of grace. Whoever starves his family is not likely to feed his neighbors.

(2) A pastor commends his people to God through faith
We commend our business to a friend when we entrust it to him. Pastors commend their friends and affairs to God by beseeching His favor toward them and believing that He will be tender toward

them. We have many fears and concerns about those whom we love and must leave. Faith eases our fears by committing them into safer hands. The burden of all the churches lies on Paul. It is heavy enough to break his back. But he places it on stronger shoulders: "Cast thy burden upon the LORD, and he shall sustain thee" (Ps. 55:22). Here is a pastor's charge and discharge. His charge is to cast his burden on God. His discharge is that God will sustain him. The apostle praises God for the grace given to the Philippians, and he prays to God for its increase: "I thank my God upon every remembrance of you, always in every prayer of mine for you all making request with joy" (Phil. 1:3–4). He enlivens his prayer with the soul of faith: "being confident of this very thing, that he which hath begun a good work in you will perform it until the day of Jesus Christ" (v. 6).

Without faith, a pastor's prayers for his people serve little purpose. There are many blessings in the womb of prayer, but the midwifery of faith must deliver them: "And all things, whatsoever ye shall ask in prayer, believing ye shall receive" (Matt. 21:22). Prayer is the key that opens God's treasury, but faith is the hand that grasps His infinite bounty. Prayer must have a promise, or else it is a vessel without a bottom. And that promise must have faith, or else the vessel is motionless. When a full gale of faith fills the sails, the vessel of prayer launches forth and returns with its richest freight.

When God acquaints Abraham with His intention to destroy Sodom, Abraham commends his nephew (who is in danger) to God by faith and prayer (Gen. 18:23). God remembers Abraham and delivers Lot out of Sodom (Gen. 19:29). Abraham's prayer hits the mark, but it is the eye of faith that aims the arrow. Faith honors God by committing to Him so great a trust as the inestimable souls of His people. God honors faith by being true to His trust. He who prays for himself and not others is like a porcupine, which wraps itself in its soft fur while turning its bristles to the world.

To sum up, when a pastor commends his people to God, he open their cases and conditions to Him in prayer, beseeching Him to relieve their needs and believing He will do so through Christ.

2. Why a Pastor Commends His People to God

In the next place, I come to the reasons why a pastor must commend his people to God. There are three.

(1) The Lord's propriety

God is the most able, loving, and faithful friend. No one is as fit to take care of a child as his father. An animal will risk its life to defend its own. The hen will hazard a duel with the hawk in order to protect her chicks. The blessed Christ gives this reason why He commends His church to God: "I pray for them: I pray not for the world, but for them which thou hast given me; for they are thine" (John 17:9). He does not pray for strangers or enemies, but God's people—those whom He has chosen, called, and loved. They are His—His treasure, portion, temple, and children.

Some people will give anything to keep their houses in good repair. Ownership is sufficient grounds for special protection. By a general providence, God takes care of His creatures. He feeds the young ravens and satisfies the hungry sparrows. In this way, He is the Preserver of people and animals. By a special providence, God takes care of His people. The saints are His—a peculiar people. Therefore, He exercises a peculiar protection over them. He is like a bird, watching over her nest (Isa. 31:5). Surely, He takes care of His own. Ownership gives rise to all the labor in the world. If all things were held in common, everyone would be careless. Because it is their property, people fertilize, plough, sow, and reap. Because it is their wealth, people work hard to increase it. God owns His people. He owns them by election—He chose them before they were born. He owns them by redemption—He paid an infinite price for them. He owns them by regeneration—He caused them to be born again. He owns them by promise: "I sware unto thee, and entered into a covenant with thee…and thou becamest mine" (Ezek. 16:8). Again, "I will be their God, and they shall be my people" (Ezek. 37:27). Because they are His, they go to Him for protection: "I am thine, save me" (Ps. 119:94). He affords them His special and gracious presence: "Israel was holiness unto the Lord, and the firstfruits of his increase. All that devour him shall offend; evil shall come upon them" (Jer. 2:3). No one can harm God's people without suffering the consequences.

(2) The world's enmity
The sheep need dogs to defend them from the wolves, which seek to devour them. Those who have many and mighty enemies need strong and faithful friends. This is another reason why Christ commends His disciples to God: "I have given them thy word, and the world hath hated them, because they are not of the world, even as I am not of the world" (John 17:14). Christ asks His Father to keep His children because they are in the midst of a wicked world. What will become of precious lambs in the midst of ravenous lions if God does not protect them?

The old enmity between the serpent and the woman has not yet worn out (Gen. 3:15). There are natural antipathies between some creatures, but there is a greater antipathy between the seed of the woman and the seed of the serpent: "An unjust man is an abomination to the just: And he that is upright in the way is an abomination to the wicked" (Prov. 29:27). The godly man hates the ungodly man's sins, but not his person. He loathes the poison, but not the cup in which it is found. Like a tender physician, he hates the disease but pities the patient. But the ungodly man hates the godly man with a hatred of perfect enmity, wishing evil to his person, and seeking it to the utmost of his power. Those who are born of the flesh persecute those who are born of the Spirit (Gal. 4:29). Their rage is so great that, if their power were equal to their malice, they would cut off Israel from being a people.

Like David, every Christian can say, "They that hate me without a cause are more than the hairs of mine head" (Ps. 69:4). The world has no just cause to hate and curse God's people. The reason for their rage, wrath, enmity, and cruelty against the saints is the fact that they are saints. Why did Cain murder his brother? "Because his own works were evil, and his brother's righteous" (1 John 3:12). The light is burdensome to owls and bats—all night creatures. Similarly, the light of a saint's holiness is offensive to the ungodly, who are accustomed to deeds of darkness. The greater the light, the more pain it causes to their eyes. Those who are unclean, and delight to wallow in the mire of vice, hate the fragrant perfume of grace.

If saints fight against powerful enemies, they require the leadership of one who is exceedingly strong. God is engaged to help His people, because the world hates them for His sake. A king counts it a dishonor to forsake the man, who has risked life and lost limb in his cause.

(3) The people's impotency
They are not able to take care of themselves. In common law, if parents die, there are officers to take care of their children. Orphans need a guardian because they cannot survive alone. The strongest Christian is but a child. Unless God holds him in His right hand, he will suffer falls and blows every day. The greatest saint cannot stand any longer than he is held. He is like a newborn infant who is ready to perish unless someone takes care of him (Ezek. 16:5).

The saints' defense must be the almighty and eternal God: "we have no might against this great company that cometh against us… but our eyes are upon thee" (2 Chron. 20:12). They cannot even perform everyday actions without God's assistance: "for in him we live, and move, and have our being" (Acts 17:28). They live in Him, move by Him, and have their beings from Him. If the spring fails, the stream dries up. If God withholds His influence, people fall to the ground.

When spiritual perils overtake the saints, they cannot stand without God's protection. When Hezekiah is left alone for a little while, he discovers the pride in his heart (2 Chron. 32:24–31). Peter seems to be a resolute and valiant man, but he flees like a coward (Matt. 26:69–75). The weak breath of a girl blows down the strong castle of his confidence. When God departs from Samson, his strength also departs (Judges 16:20). The holiest man is no match for the devil. If God leaves him, his defense is gone.

The ability to perform sacred duties comes from God: "not that we are sufficient of ourselves to think any thing as of ourselves; but our sufficiency is of God" (2 Cor. 3:5). We consider the act of thinking to be an easy thing. Yet, unless God helps us, it is too hard for us. God must give fresh supplies of His Spirit in every duty, or else

His people cannot rightly perform them. Their greatest fullness is not the fullness of a fountain, but of a vessel. It is always pouring out and, therefore, must always be taking in. The conduit, which is continually running, must receive water continually from the river.

Habitual grace lies like water at the bottom of a pump. We cannot get it until God pours in His exciting grace. This is implied in Christ's petition to His Father: "Holy Father, keep through thine own name those whom thou hast given me" (John 17:11). They are poor and helpless children, who cannot stand on their own. They are pitiful and helpless creatures. Without God's protection, they lose the grace which Christ purchased for them and bestowed upon them, and fall into sin. Therefore, Christ prays.

Application
Having explained the text, I proceed to its application.

1. It Reveals the Piety of a True Pastor
Like the apostle, true pastors commend their people to God. This is their character. Some people's mouths are full of poison. Their tongues are black with blasphemies against God and His people. But faithful pastors speak a different language. As they are blessed men, so they are men who bless. Some pastors are ministers of Satan— their business is to accuse the brothers. While God's people pity them and pray for them, they return blessing with cursing. But true pastors seek and study their people's welfare. The false mother did not care if the boy was killed and divided. But the true mother cried out "for her bowels yearned upon her son" (1 Kings 3:26).

Pastors are fathers, and their people are their children. Wicked pastors are false fathers, who do not care what becomes of their children. The great murderer of souls might seek to kill them, and they will not speak out against him. Far too often, they help him drive the poor sheep out of their pasture into his slaughterhouse. But godly pastors, like true fathers, seek their children's welfare. They cry out with Hagar: "Let me not see the death of the child" (Gen. 21:16). They cannot bear to witness the eternal death of their poor, carnal, ignorant neighbors. Godly pastors open their hearts and mouths to God on behalf of their people: "Lord, some of the unregenerate children, whom Thou hast committed to my charge, stand at the point of death. I have acquainted them with the end and evil of their wicked ways, but I cannot obtain a sober hearing. Lord, if Thou wert to speak to them, they would listen. Thou canst open their eyes and break their hearts. Lord, come down quickly, or else my children die eternally."

2. It Displays the Privilege of a Gracious People
The apostle commends his people to God. Although earthly friends might leave them, their heavenly Father will never leave them. Christ prays for them in heaven, and Christians pray for them on earth. It is the Christian's joy to know that he is in his brothers' prayers.

Man's joy is bound up in God's favor. Therefore, to be commended to God's care must be a great comfort. There is no greater privilege. Israel enjoys such a favored condition: "For what nation is there so great, who hath God so nigh unto them, as the LORD our God is in all things that we call upon him for?" (Deut. 4:7). From Israel's outward condition, we might question how she is greater than all the nations of the earth. The people wander in a desolate wilderness without food for their bellies or clothing for their bodies. If bread had not fallen from heaven, they would have died of hunger. If water had not flowed from the rock, they would have died of thirst. If their clothes had not lasted, they would have been naked. They do not have houses, but tents. Wherever they turn, they face the paws of ravenous beasts and the hands of cruel men.

Even so, no nation can compare with Israel for honor and happiness. Why? God is their patron and guardian. Other nations might excel Israel in number, treasure, and livestock. Other nations might possess greater honors and pleasures. Yet every nation is inferior, because none has God so near. A nation without God experiences long dismal nights and sharp bitter frosts, no matter what else it enjoys.

When the Scripture says that people are obnoxious, it means that God has forsaken them: "I have forsaken mine house, I have left mine heritage; I have given the dearly beloved of my soul into the hand of her enemies" (Jer. 12:7). What is the result of God forsaking His house? It tumbles down. "I have given the dearly beloved of my soul into the hand of her enemies." He adds, "Many pastors have destroyed my vineyard, they have trodden my portion under foot, they have made my pleasant portion a desolate wilderness" (v. 10). When the fence is removed, the vineyard is quickly destroyed.

When David prays against the church's enemies, what does he request? "Let them be confounded and put to shame" (Ps. 35:4). That is to say, let them be disappointed in their plans. It is terrible to labor with sorrow and difficulty, yet produce nothing. David adds, "Let them be as chaff before the wind: and let the angel of the LORD chase them" (v. 5). That is to say, let them perish speedily, suddenly, and permanently. David's first request is bad, but this one is worse. The next is worst of all: "Let their way be dark and slippery: and let the angel of the LORD persecute them" (v. 6). David knows that to be out of God's care is to be under God's curse. That will make his enemies miserable indeed. A solar eclipse darkens all creation, even though other heavenly lights shine brightly. Similarly, the loss of God is exceedingly woeful, even when earthly comforts remain. Some people have large estates but no God. Others have high privileges but no God. Still others have excellent accomplishments but no God. This lack of God clouds all other comforts.

In marked contrast, the enjoyment of God is the greatest favor. God puts beauty and glory on the soul of whomever He approaches. Because the favorable testimony of an adversary is of great worth, let Balaam give his evidence: "How goodly are thy tents, O Jacob, and thy tabernacles, O Israel" (Num. 24:5). Here, he speaks by way of admiration. Their tents and encampments are so lovely that they affect him. Why does Balaam see Israel as incomparable? Why does he admire her order, glory, and beauty? "The LORD his God is with him, and the shout of a king is among them" (Num. 23:21).

The new temple, which the Spirit of God describes in its various dimensions and perfections, derives all its glory from God's gracious presence: "and the name of the city from that day shall be, the LORD is there" (Ezek. 48:35).

God seems to make Israel a gracious offer:

> And the LORD said unto Moses, Depart, and go up hence, thou and the people which thou hast brought up out of the land of Egypt, unto the land of which I sware unto Abraham, to Isaac, and to Jacob, saying, Unto thy seed will I give it: and I will send an angel before thee; and I will drive out the Canaanite, the Amorite, and the Hittite, and the Perizzite, the Hivite, and the Jebusite: unto a land flowing with milk and honey: for I will not go up in the midst of thee; for thou art a stiffnecked people: lest I consume thee in the way (Ex. 33:1–3).

How do the people receive God's offer? "And when the people heard these evil tidings, they mourned: and no man did put on him his ornaments" (v. 4). Why do they view God's offer as "evil tidings"? An angel will guide and guard them. He will defeat all their enemies. He will give them the best country under heaven—a land flowing with milk and honey. Surely, most people would value such an offer. So why do the Israelites mourn? None of these privileges can make up for the lack of God's presence. For this reason, Moses prays, "If thy presence go not with me, carry us not up hence" (v. 15). It is better to be in the barren wilderness with God than in bountiful Canaan without Him. The glorious angel cannot comfort them; the defeat of their enemies cannot exalt them, and the possession of the land cannot satisfy them. If God leaves them, then all the glory, honor, and happiness depart from Israel. "If thy presence go not with me, carry us not up hence." But here is the privilege of the saints: "My presence shall go with thee, and I will give thee rest" (v. 14).

3. It Provides Comfort for Those Commended to God's Care

The apostle has little to give to his sorrowful friends, but he speaks on their behalf to the King, who is able and willing to give them all things. That is his greatest act of love. By commending them to God, he opens heaven's treasury. They value Paul's prayers more than the kingdoms of the world.

Commendation

Beloved friends, it is my duty and privilege to follow the apostle's example. You are the people to whom I was first called as a pastor. Opportunities have arisen in other churches, but I have waived all thoughts of leaving you—my first love. I have been among you for eleven years. I cannot complain, for I have not spent my strength and labor in vain. Some of you have acknowledged that you are the seals of my ministry. Some have acknowledged that God has made me instrumental to your growth in grace. God's power has appeared in my weakness and His mercy in my unworthiness. That said, how many of you have heard the gospel all these years without any effect? Oh, how speechless will you be at the day of Christ! After so many years of public and private preaching, you are still in a Christ-less and grace-less condition. Surely, no one sinks so deep into hell as he who is pressed down under the weight of the gospel.

Despite my grief for some of you, I must admire the grace that has made me useful. I have enjoyed more of God in His ordinances while among you than at any other time in my life. I acknowledge that many of you have demonstrated much respect and kindness toward me—above what I deserve and above what I have heard is customary in other churches. My joy is the joy of you who fear God. But now that God's providence is separating us, I do not know how to express my love for you, except by imitating the apostle's example. I commend you to God, and to "the word of his grace."

1. Commendation to God

God is everything. If He is yours, nothing can hurt you. If He is yours, everything will help you. If someone were to ask you to whom you would like to be commended, I hope you would answer *God*. All good is in God. The covenant of grace is a rich mercy. All of the world's crowns and empires are nothing in comparison. Here is the sun, which makes heaven so glorious: "I will be to them a God, and they shall be to me a people" (Heb. 8:10). In His birth and death, the Son of God's purpose was high and honorable—to purchase those whom God had cast away because of their rebellion. "For Christ also hath once suffered for sins, the just for the unjust, that he might bring us to God" (1 Peter 3:18).

When he was in danger, David committed his soul into God's hands: "Into thine hand I commit my spirit" (Ps. 31:5). Our dying Redeemer, who knew the worth of His soul because of the price He paid for our souls, declared, "Father, into thy hands I commend my spirit" (Luke 23:46). To commend you to God is all I can do for you, and it is all you can desire from me. If you were my closest relatives (the object of my deepest affections), I could do no more (I need do no more) than to commend you to God.

(1) I commend you to God's special favor and affection
God's favor is a lump of sugar that sweetens a bitter cup. The small bird sings pleasantly in her small, soft nest, while the large bird squawks harshly in her large, thorny nest. In the soft bed of God's special love the saints sleep comfortably, while the wicked are ill at ease in their high and lofty places. God's general love is like the ordinary beams of the sun, which convey heat and light for the world's refreshment. In this way, God is good to all—His mercy is over all His works. But God's special love is like the beams of the sun magnified through a glass. They only ignite what they rest upon. God's love for His children in Christ is a burning love. He is favorable to His chosen ones: "Remember me, O LORD…that I may see the good of thy chosen" (Ps. 106:4–5).

A kiss from God is more valuable than all the kingdoms of the earth. The Christian can live happily, knowing that God favors him. In the light of a king's countenance, there is life. His favor is as refreshing as rain (Prov. 16:15). If that is true, then what does it mean to live in the light of God's countenance? God's special favor is a pearl of such worth that Christ purchased it with His blood. It is impossible to obtain anything greater. David prays, "LORD, lift thou up the light of thy countenance upon us" (Ps. 4:6). "Turn us again, O God, and cause thy face to shine; and we shall be saved" (Ps. 80:3). When we love others as ourselves, we can desire nothing better or greater for them than God's favor.

Joseph loves Benjamin: "his bowels did yearn upon his brother" (Gen. 43:30). How does he show it? What does he request for him?

"God be gracious unto thee, my son" (v. 29). Daniel fasts and prays because of the people's afflictions. When he pours out his heart to God on their behalf, he sums up his prayers in one petition: "Now therefore, O our God, hear the prayer of thy servant, and his supplications, and cause thy face to shine upon thy sanctuary that is desolate, for the Lord's sake" (Dan. 9:17). The high priest's prayer for the people has the same goal: "the LORD make his face shine upon thee, and be gracious unto thee" (Num. 6:25). Paul utters the same request on behalf of the Corinthians: "The grace of the Lord Jesus Christ, and the love of God, and the communion of the Holy Ghost, be with you all. Amen" (2 Cor. 13:14).

I commend you to this God, whose favor is life (Ps. 30), and whose loving-kindness is better than life (Ps. 43). My prayer for you will always be: "God be merciful unto us, and bless us; and cause his face to shine upon us" (Ps. 67:1).

(2) I commend you to God's special care and protection

The saints are always within the view of God's favorable eye, and under the guard of His almighty arm (Isa. 27:4). He keeps them as the apple of His eye (Zech. 2:8). God's providence extends to all His creatures. But, in a special manner, it is operative for the safety of His saints: He "is the Savior of all men *[that is, in respect of their temporal salvation—preservation]*, specially of those that believe" (1 Tim. 4:10). The godly are like wheat, and the ungodly are like chaff. Good farmers do not spoil the chaff, but they give careful attention to the wheat. When fire breaks out, God might leave sinners to be consumed, but He makes certain that His saints (His jewels) are saved. The church is God's house; therefore, He guards it. "For the eyes of the LORD run to and fro throughout the whole earth, to shew himself strong in the behalf of them whose heart is perfect toward him" (2 Chron. 16:9). This verse affirms two truths.

First, it affirms the universality of God's providence: His eyes "run to and fro throughout the whole earth." According to mythology, Diana's temple was destroyed when she was busy at Alexander's birth. She could not be in two places at once. But God is present in all places at all times. Therefore, He is never absent from His church, which is His temple. Heaven is God's palace, but not His prison.

Second, it affirms the efficacy of God's providence: "to shew himself strong." God fights with His eyes and hands. He sees His people's danger, and saves them from it. God always watches and protects His people. If God were to forsake His people, every enemy would quickly find them: "They are bread for us: their defense is departed from them" (Num. 14:9). The deer that emerge from the forest are shot, while those that remain in the forest are safe. When God left the Israelites, even for a little while, they were naked (Ex. 32:25). Why? It was not from a lack of clothes or weapons but from a lack of God's presence and protection.

You are safe while God remains with you. If trials and troubles come, hide under the shelter of this shield. If He does not prevent the evil of affliction, He will protect you from the evil in affliction. God is a strong tower (Prov. 18:10), which no cannon can penetrate. He is a high tower (Ps. 18:2), which no ladder can scale. He is a refuge for the oppressed saint and a help in time of trouble.

I commend you to this God, whose power is a sufficient shelter and whose providence is a sure protection. He governs all creatures in heaven and earth. He has infinite wisdom to direct you and infinite strength to support you. My prayer for you is this: "The LORD…preserve thee from all evil…preserve thy soul…preserve thy going out and thy coming in from this time forth, and even for evermore" (Ps. 121:7–8).

(3) I commend you to God's universal benediction
I commend you to God's blessing in all your endeavors—His grace to comfort you in the midst of the world's hatred, His power to protect you in the midst of hardship, and His presence to prosper you in all the works of your hands. The earth's fruitfulness depends on heaven's influence. If the sun withholds its heat and the clouds withhold their rain, everything withers. Likewise, the success of your actions depends on God's blessing. If He denies His concurrence, nothing prospers. "Except the LORD build the house, they labor in vain that build it" (Ps. 127:1). It is pointless to maintain the house

that God chooses to tear down or plough the field that God chooses to make desolate. Some philosophers tell us that God is the soul of the world. As the soul is in every part of the body, so God is in every part of the world. The body cannot move unless the soul animates it. Likewise, nothing in the world can move unless God enlivens it. He sets everything in motion.

It is said of David that he prospered wherever Saul sent him (1 Chron. 11:9). But what was the cause of his success? "The LORD of hosts was with him." It is God's gracious presence that gives success to every endeavor. God's blessing can turn water into wine—temporal mercies into spiritual benefits. He can turn poison into wholesome food. He can turn every stone, cast by your enemies, into a precious stone. He can cause man's wrath to work for His praise and your profit. While wicked people plot against God's people, the wise and powerful God causes them to conspire for His people. The world's actions are against the saints intentionally according to the malice of their hearts, but the actions ultimately work for the saints according to God's overruling hand. The scorching sun of persecution ripens God's people for a glorious harvest.

I commend you to this God who can blow on His enemies' plans, causing them to perish, and breathe on His people's actions, causing them to prosper. He can order all His providences to tend to your spiritual profit and eternal peace. My prayer for you is this: "The LORD hear thee in the day of trouble; the name of the God of Jacob defend thee; send thee help from the sanctuary, and strengthen thee out of Zion.... Grant thee according to thine own heart, and fulfill all thy counsel" (Ps. 20:1–2, 4).

(4) I commend you to God, who is a great friend

For your further comfort, understand that this God is an able friend, loving friend, and faithful friend. Therefore, to commend you to Him is the greatest good I can do for you.

First, God is the most able friend. A friend at court is a great benefit because he is able to influence the king. What does it mean to have God (who commands all things) as our friend? God is able to do more for you than you can ask or think. Thirty times in the book of Job, He is called *Almighty*. He can do more than we can express or conceive. He made the whole world out of nothing. What is beyond His ability to do for you? He is able to defend you from whatever is hurtful. With a mere breath, God can blast all His enemies' plans and persons. How happy are those who have Him for their stronghold! God is pleased to call Himself the watchman of His people. He is a watchman who never slumbers or sleeps. His eyes never close. All His thoughts are for the good of His people. If enemies come before or behind His people, He is the Lord of hosts. He is their defense. While He is present, they are safe.

Are you in physical danger? God can deflect the blows, and no evil can touch you without His permission. All His servants are privileged persons, and He can make a hedge about you and your house (Job 1:10). When He does, neither people nor demons can penetrate to injure you. If affliction is near, God will not be far away. "When thou passest through the waters, I will be with thee; And through the rivers, they shall not overflow thee: When thou walkest through the fire, thou shalt not be burned; Neither shall the flame kindle upon thee" (Isa. 43:2). If the church were a burning bush, it would not be consumed because God is in it, making it safe in the fire.

It is also safe in the water. If it is tossed up and down by tempestuous winds and boisterous waves, and ready to sink, Christ is in it. Although He appears to sleep, He is merely waiting for a fit opportunity to manifest and magnify His power (Mark 4:38–39). When the storm comes, He awakens, and with a word, calms the sea. The church is tossed, but never drowned. "God is in the midst of her; she shall not be moved; God shall help her, and that right early" (Ps. 46:5). God is said to ride "upon the heaven" to help His people (Deut. 33:26–27). That might mean He comes speedily to deliver His people. It might also mean He commands His creatures to be serviceable to His people's safety. As a man can command a horse with a bit, so the omnipotent God can command the heavens for His people's benefit.

Are you in spiritual danger? God is able to defend you. The world is a slippery place, but He is able to keep you from falling

(Jude 24). We are apt to fall on the right hand through the world's allurements, and on the left hand through the world's afflictions. Those who travel over rugged terrain often fall, but God is able to keep you from falling. If God keeps hold of you, you will stay on course. By His power, He guards us "through faith unto a salvation ready to be revealed in the last time" (1 Peter 1:5). His power and love are the eagles' wings upon which the saints are carried out of Egypt through the wilderness to Canaan.

He can keep you from falling in two ways. First, He can keep you from temptation and does so, when He sees it will be too hard for you. Not everyone has the same faith; therefore, God does not test everyone in the same fire. He is acquainted with the strongest soldiers in His army, and He calls them to the hardest service (Rev. 3:10). When the weather is bad, He does not allow His small child to go outside. Second, He can enable you to defeat the tempter. Little David conquers great Goliath. Joseph is not so much as singed by the great fire which his master's wife set for him. Daniel emerges from the lion's den as safe as when he entered. The goldsmith would not put his gold in the fire if he knew it would be consumed. Man is no match for the devil, but God is more than a match.

"Lord," says Augustine, "when I had a heart to sin, Thou didst keep me from temptation, and when I had temptation, Thou didst keep my heart from sin." If your heart is as dry as tinder, God can prevent Satan from striking a match. If God does permit Satan to strike a match, He can still prevent the tinder from igniting. He is able to defend you from what is hurtful, and relieve you with what is needful. God knows you are helpless, but He can send you all that you require. God's estate is infinite; therefore, He is able to provide for all His children. I know you desire (above all the world) proficiency of grace and perfection in glory. He can build you up in grace, and He can cause all grace to abound. If this sun draws near to you, the fruit of the Spirit will ripen apace. This well of salvation can fill every vessel of your heart, no matter how wide.

God can make the infant in grace to grow until he becomes a young man, a strong man, and a father. God can give you an inheritance that fades not away and lead you through all your hardships. He can crown you with heaven, where you will be kept from sin and suffering, where you will be free from all fighting, where you will never doubt His love, where you will never offend others with your purity, where you will never need to defend yourself from injury, where all tears will be wiped from your eyes, where persecutors will cease from troubling you, where the weary will be at rest, and where your name will be vindicated, your infirmities banished, your graces perfected, and your soul blessed. You will be locked up in Christ's bosom and lodged in God's embrace forever.

Second, God is the most loving friend. God has power to enable Him—and love to move Him—to do good to His people. Jonathan risks a great deal for David's safety because he loves him as his own soul (1 Sam. 20:30–34). Those who are the object of God's love are sure of His helping hand. He chooses His love and then loves His choice. He had precious thoughts of His people before they had any thoughts of themselves. God loves His people because they are His eternal choice. The mother loves the child she carried for nine months in her womb. Oh, how God loves His people, whom He carried in the womb of His purpose from all eternity. He loves them as they are His own image—they are like Him in grace and holiness. He loves them for resembling Him in holiness. Grace is lovely. God cannot but love His saints, because He loves Himself.

God loves His people, because they are His Son's purchase. That which is so dearly bought is not easily hated. Jacob was exceedingly tender toward Benjamin. He could expose his ten sons to foul weather, but he did not want the wind to so much as blow on Benjamin. What is the cause of Jacob's extraordinary affection? Benjamin was the child of his beloved Rachel, and he was dearly bought—he cost the life of Jacob's dear wife (Gen. 35:16–18). God loves His saints with a singular love because they are the children of His dear Son—the travail of His soul. These children caused God's beloved Son much pain and anguish and cost Him His very life.

God loves His children more than the whole world. They are His gold in the midst of dross, and He establishes the world as a tent in which His children dwell during their pilgrimage. When God transfers them to His house, He will take down this tent. God loves them as His own Son (John 17:26–27). Who can know the love that God has for His Son? He has the same love for His saints. His name is love; His nature is love; His Son is the token of His love; His Spirit is the earnest of His love; and the gospel is His love letter.

For this reason, those who are committed to God's keeping are happy. While they might suffer, God sympathizes with them and supports them, and the tender Father proportions the burden to the strength of their backs. His children are like a stringed instrument. He does not let the strings be too slack lest they ruin the music, nor does He let them be too tight lest they break. He will not allow His people to be afflicted above what they are able to bear (1 Cor. 10:13).

God's love sets all His other attributes to work for His people's good. His wisdom plans, His power acts, and His faithfulness completes all that He promises for the comfort of His church. He does all this because He loves them. What would David not have done for Absalom, whom he loved so dearly? When Absalom rebelled, David's heart relented towards Absalom out of love. What a charge he gives to his captains concerning him! "Deal gently for my sake with the young man, even with Absalom" (2 Sam. 18:5). What will God not do for His chosen ones, whom He loves? When they wander away from Him, He follows them and woos them. "For the iniquity of his covetousness was I wroth, and smote him: I hid me, and was wroth, and he went on forwardly in the way of his heart" (Isa. 57:17). Here is a child caught in a great crime. His father corrects him. But instead of kissing the rod, the child kicks at the hand that holds it. What is the fruit of such rebellion? We might expect greater severity. But what does love do? "I have seen his ways, and will heal him: I will lead him also, and restore comforts unto him and to his mourners" (Isa. 57:18). Although he is disobedient, he is God's child. God will throw away His rod, and draw His children with the cord of love.

Third, God is the most faithful friend. God's love is constant. Some people love for a time, but their love is like a candle—it burns in calm weather but extinguishes in a stormy wind. But God is an everlasting friend. His love is like the sun—it can never be extinguished and always shines in full strength. "A friend loveth at all times, and a brother is born for adversity" (Prov. 17:17). God is such a friend. He never fails to appear on behalf of His suffering servants (2 Tim. 4:16–17). The ancients pictured friendship in the shape of a handsome young man, bearing this inscription: *to live and die with you, summer and winter, far and near.* God is such a friend. He never disowns or denies His people. In the fiery furnace, the three young men enjoyed His presence (Dan. 3:9–30).

People are mutable. They use their friends like sun dials—they only regard them when the sun shines on them. But God is "a faithful Creator" (1 Peter 4:19). He watches over the house He builds—especially when it needs repair and is in danger of falling. Many people are like ponds—clear at the top, but muddy at the bottom. That is to say, their words are pleasant, but their hearts are corrupt. But God is a faithful friend. He never fails His children. He is a physician, who is sure to visit His patients when they are sick.

God is faithful to His promise. His Word is the truth (Col. 1:5). His church is the pillar of the truth (1 Tim. 3:15); His sacraments are the seals of the truth; and He is the God of truth (Ps. 31:5). When He promises, we have no reason to fear because God keeps His promise to a word. "Ye know in all your hearts and in all your souls, that not one thing hath failed of all the good things which the LORD your God spake concerning you" (Josh. 23:14). God's promise is equivalent to possession. He delivered Israel after 430 years in Egypt, as He promised (Ex. 12:41). He delivered the remnant after seventy years in Babylon, as He promised (Dan. 5:30). God's promises are intended to refresh you in fainting hours; as God's love is the root upon which they grow, so His faithfulness is the hand that brings them to you. It is your happiness that your riches lie in God's good hands. You can be confident—God will not suffer a liar to enter heaven, and He will not suffer a lie to enter His own heart. "Faithful is he that calleth you, who also will do it" (1 Thess. 5:24).

Therefore, my dearly beloved, I commend you to God's favor and affection, power and protection, care and benediction. He is an able, loving, and faithful friend. As I commend you to God in prayer, I trust that you will do the same for me. "Now I beseech you, brethren, for the Lord Jesus Christ's sake, and for the love of the Spirit, that ye strive together with me in your prayers to God for me" (Rom. 15:30).

2. Commendation to the "Word of God's Grace"

As I have commended you to God, so let me commend you to the "word of his grace." You have great cause to value the "word of God's grace." The law breathes forth a cold gale, a north wind of threats, but the gospel breathes forth a warm gale, a south wind of promises. Of all God's attributes, we must not neglect His grace. For Christ's sake, and for your soul's sake, I beg you to value the gospel. What are we without it? We are condemned criminals—liable to be displayed as monuments of God's fury in hell. Every person who faces execution esteems a pardon, so surely, we have cause to prize the gospel. We would still be imprisoned under the law's curse, in the dungeon of endless wrath and misery, if the gospel had not opened the prison doors, broken our chains, and freed our souls. I commend the "word of his grace" to you for four reasons.

(1) It will purify your heart

I know you need grace. The word of grace can impart and increase grace. It is the usual pipe through which God conveys grace to the heart. Civil laws might reform your actions, but only the gospel can renew your affections. Some poets speak of musicians who can tame savage animals with their music. The word of God's grace can do much more. It can turn stones into Abraham's children and change a heart of stone into a heart of flesh. It can tame lions and turn them into lambs (Isa. 11:4–6).

You should desire the word of grace to come with power to your soul. You should desire not only to hear it but to savor it—not only to read it but to relish it. Oh, my friends, the lack of this is the undoing of thousands. Why do some people who seem bound for heaven fall away? The reason is this: the gospel never captures the royal fort of their hearts. Although they have some knowledge of it, they never love it. Therefore, let me beseech you not to receive "the grace of God in vain" (2 Cor. 6:1). How sad will it be for you if your heart is like a rock on which the dews of grace fall without making an impression! The apricot tree leans on the wall, but it is rooted in the earth. Likewise, some people seem to lean on Christ, but they are still rooted in their lusts.

If grace is your enemy, you have no friend in heaven or earth. The fruit of trees, standing in the sun, ripens fast. So too, the sins of people who stand in the sunshine of the gospel are great. If the gospel is not a morning star to you, ushering in the sun of righteousness upon you, it will be an evening star to you, bringing an everlasting night of death and darkness upon you. As the ocean sees some ships safely to port while sinking others, so the word of God's grace is either a savor of life unto life or a savor of death unto death.

(2) It will govern your life
Your whole walk must be regular, and there is no other rule to walk by than the word of God's grace: "as many as walk according to this rule" (Gal. 6:16)—that is, according to the gospel. It contains promises to comfort you and precepts to challenge you. Therefore, it is called a "royal law" (James 2:8). It is a law because it is the canon of our lives, adopted by Christ into the family of the gospel. It is a royal law because God, the King of the world, gave it to us. He has sovereignty and dominion over all and power to command whatever He pleases. The "word of his grace" is a royal law because it is the King's highway, and we wander from it under the penalty of rebellion. Indeed, the gospel is a law of liberty but not of licentiousness (James 1:25). It frees us from the curse—but not the commands—of the law. A true Christian is not without the law but under the law to Christ (1 Cor. 9:21).

Make it your rule for faith. The gospel is the only creed, and whoever believes it is a true believer. The Word, Christ, is the personal foundation for every Christian; likewise, the word of God's grace is the doctrinal foundation for every Christian (Eph. 2:19–20).

"Thus we believe," says Tertullian, "when we first believe that we ought to believe nothing beyond the Scriptures." Paul proved himself to be a true believer, because he believed all things written in the law and prophets (Acts 24:14).

Make it your rule for worship. To serve God according to your own inventions or prescriptions is rebellion, and as the rust corrupts the iron, apocryphal worship corrupts evangelical worship (Matt. 15:7). All worship without biblical warrant is like counterfeit currency—treason against the King of Heaven. God charged Jeroboam with this crime: "So he offered upon the altar which he had made…in the month which he had devised of his own heart" (1 Kings 12:33) because Jeroboam took liberty to worship wherever and whenever he pleased.

Man is not his own maker; therefore, he has no right to be his own lawgiver. He is entirely dependent on God and must obey God's laws. The gospel is not only a royal law, but a perfect law (James 1:25). It does not require any additions or traditions to correct its defects, and it is a horrid blasphemy to suggest that the Scripture is deficient. Christ was faithful "in all [God's] house" (Heb. 3:2). This would have been impossible if the laws had been insufficient for God's service. Therefore, those who seek to add to His Word are saying (not explicitly, but implicitly) that Christ was an unfaithful Prophet. Friends, I beg you to keep close to this rule. When inferior goods fill the shops, we must test them in the light: "To the law and to the testimony" (Isa. 8:20).

In all things, live by the gospel and look to the gospel. Let it be a light to your feet and a lantern to your path. Keep the Word, and in an hour of temptation it will keep you from sinning, and in an hour of affliction it will keep you from sinking. When in doubt, the lawyer consults his Littleton, the doctor his Hippocrates, and the philosopher his Aristotle. But the godly must always take counsel from the gospel. "Ponder the path of thy feet, and let all thy ways be established. Turn not to the right hand nor to the left: Remove thy feet from evil" (Prov. 4:26–27). Let the law of God be your counselor. Fear whatever God's law does not allow.

The chick not only fears the hawk, but runs away when she sees its shadow. Do not turn away from God's law in the least matter. Hate the appearance—and shun the occasion—of evil. Many people work hard to save their money and maintain their credit. You must labor to guard your conscience and save your soul.

(3) It will give support in opposition
The gospel is an armory that supplies Christians with spiritual weapons in their holy war against the kingdom of darkness. All other armor, such as ability and morality, is (as Alexander said of the richly clothed Persians when they entered the field of battle) prey to the enemy rather than a defense to the soldier. First, the "word of his grace" is a shield against evil principles (Matt. 22:29) and may be fitly called, as some called Augustine, the hammer of heresy. Whoever is mighty in Scripture can hit this unclean bird in the eye, wounding it mortally with one blow (Acts 18:28). With this sword in their hands, Christians have encountered men of great learning, disarmed them of all their philosophical weaponry, and foiled them.

Second, the "word of his grace" is a shield against evil practices. "Wherewithal shall a young man cleanse his way? By taking heed thereto according to thy word" (Ps. 119:9). What can rein in a young man who is hot and heady, galloping at full speed down the road of sin and hell? The gospel can do it. He is busy tasting and enjoying his carnal pleasures, but when he tastes the sweetness of the gospel, he will forsake his carnal pleasure as coarse food.

Does Satan assault you? You must use the gospel for your defense. Our blessed Savior does not use His deity to drive away the devil, but fights against him with the Word (Rev. 12:11). He does so, in order to show us how to handle this weapon (Matt. 4:4, 7, 10).

Does the world entrap you? It is a place of thorns and briars (2 Cor. 10:4). Therefore, you must shod your feet with "the preparation of the gospel of peace" (Eph. 6:15), and you will walk comfortably through the world. Apparently, the Irish run so lightly on the ground that they can cross over bogs, in which others sink. Many people perish in the world's quagmires because their feet are not shod with the gospel.

Does the world allure you with prosperity? This is extremely dangerous bait. Adam fell in paradise, while Job conquered on the dunghill. When the oyster fears the crab, it closes its shell and is safe. But when the oyster is without fear, it opens itself up to the sun, thereby making itself vulnerable to the crab's claws. When we look into the other world, we discover that this world is nothing in comparison. Moses looked to the reward and, therefore, scorned the dignity of being the son of Pharaoh's daughter (Heb. 11:24–25).

Does the world frighten you with adversity? The gospel shows us that the cross is the pathway to the crown. As long as the traveler to a glorious kingdom is on the right way, he is content. Christ went to Jerusalem (the vision of peace) by way of Bethany (the house of grief). As Martin Luther says, "Every saint must be a sufferer." I hope you are willing to go to heaven in the same way Christ and His saints have gone. The gospel holds your head above these storms by showing you the gain you receive through affliction. Like some creatures, Christians see best in the night of sorrow and distress. When there is no wind, the chaff remains with the wheat; but when the wind blows, it removes the chaff. The word of God's grace will assure you of divine supplies suitable to your sufferings. Like a caring mother, God will tend to His sick children. There is no greater joy in the world than what is found under the cross. Israel never saw so much of God as in the wilderness—manna from heaven, a pillar before them, and a rock behind them.

(4) It will give comfort in affliction

The ram's skin protected the ark from harsh weather, and it typifies the gospel's defense of the church. David says his comfort in affliction is that God's Word has quickened him (Ps. 119:107). When the weight of his affliction was ready to sink him, the gospel preserved him from sinking. If God's precepts are sweeter than the honey and the honeycomb, how sweet are His promises? If God's statutes are the saint's song, then surely the "word of his grace" is the saint's triumph. This Word affords you exceedingly precious promises whereby you are welcomed as the friends of God, the members of Christ, the temples of the Spirit, and the heirs of heaven. The promise brings comfort to a broken heart when it is ready to die with despair: "that we through patience and comfort of the scriptures might have hope" (Rom. 15:4).

This life would be little better than hell if not for the hope of heaven. The hope of future happiness as discovered in the gospel will (like the bobble to the fishing line) keep your heart above all waters of affliction. At present, you have a storm; but one day, you will have an everlasting calm. At present, you are tossed to and fro; but faith sees the distant land. Without question, this sight will support and strengthen your heart. When trouble comes, be careful not to seek comfort from any of the creatures. They are mere puddles of water. The "word of his grace" is the pure river of the water of life. It is as clear as crystal. This river makes glad the city of God.

Conclusion

In conclusion, I hope your treasure, wealth, honor, and happiness are found in this: God is our friend. According to my power, I commend you to this God—His favor and singular affection, His power and special protection, His care and universal benediction. I cannot commend you to anyone so faithful. Others fall like leaves in autumn, but God will never leave you nor forsake you.

I cannot commend you to anyone so loving. He lived in love and died for love, and His love is like Himself—boundless and bottomless. I cannot commend you to anyone so able. He can meet all your needs and fill your soul to the brim. He can edify you, and give you an inheritance where all the heirs are kings and queens and where you will reign with Christ forever with a robe of purity on your back, a palm of victory in your hand, a crown of glory on your head, and a song of triumph in your mouth. There, you will gather together to worship Him without fear and drink freely of His sweetest favor. There, your service will be without the smallest sin, and your soul without the least sorrow.

There, pastors and their people will meet and never separate. It is some comfort to know that, although we are in different places, we can meet together at the throne of grace. But what a comfort to know that we will meet together in the palace of glory! But since we must part here: "And now brethren, I commend you to God, and to the word of his grace, which is able to build you up, and to give you an inheritance among all them which are sanctified."

Afterword

I began this book by expressing my desire to see a generation of *Pauline* pastors—men with a clear sense of their calling, coupled with an insatiable desire to please God. Here's an interesting (and somewhat revealing) question: How do you think people would respond to the apostle Paul, if he were to seek pastoral employment in our day?[1]

For starters, many people would be offended by Paul's personality (1 Cor. 2:1–3). By his own admission, he wasn't a very charismatic sort of man. He wasn't particularly engaging or compelling. He wasn't antisocial, yet at the same time he wasn't chiefly concerned about social networking. He didn't accept everyone regardless of how they reasoned or behaved. I imagine most people today would view Paul's personality as a serious threat to the supreme goal of cultivating an accepting and welcoming church environment.

Many people would be scandalized by Paul's insistence on church discipline (1 Cor. 5:2–5). He was intolerant of those who indulged in doctrinal defection or moral deviance and was in the habit of confronting and rebuking such people. He actually handed people over to Satan, if they refused to repent of their sin, viewing this as absolutely necessary and an expression of love. By today's standards, Paul's insistence on moral purity and doctrinal fidelity would be labeled unloving, and people would dismiss him as judgmental.

---

1. David Wells asks this question in *No Place for Truth*, 290–91. Much of what follows in this section is adapted from Wells.

Many people would be insulted by Paul's refusal to accept the legitimacy of each person's private views (1 Tim. 1:18–20). He was adamant in his insistence that God gives truth objectively in Christ. He was committed to Scripture—not some perceived voice in the back of his head. In the midst of moral and philosophical relativism, he was unwavering in his proclamation of God's Word. By today's standards, Paul's commitment to absolute truth would seem arrogant, and many people would view him as out of touch.

Many people would be confused by Paul's preaching. He seldom told stories; he wasn't culturally hip; he never gave practical, "how-to" seminars, and he preached sermons that lasted more than twenty minutes. He continually expounded Old Testament promises and wasn't guided by the latest headlines, philosophies, cultural trends, or world events. By today's standards, his preaching skills would be seen as severely lacking—his preaching would be viewed as boring .

Finally, many people would be agitated by Paul's theological focus. He defined all things according to God's glory—not man's happiness. He insisted on explaining difficult theological concepts and on using terms unknown to his audience. He viewed the knowledge of God as an end in itself—after all, what could be more practical and beneficial than knowing God? By today's standards, he would seem too theoretical and impractical.

Perspective is a strange thing. Often, what's great in the world's eyes is small in God's eyes. The opposite is also true—what's great in God's eyes is often small in the world's eyes. If we aren't careful, we can easily slip into the world's way of thinking and allow the world's values to shape our perspective—even our perspective of pastoral ministry.

That being said, the prevailing condition within today's church isn't all doom and gloom—not by any means. But it does pose a growing challenge to pastors who desire to be faithful to their calling. In 2 Timothy 4:5, Paul charges Timothy: "But watch thou in all things, endure afflictions, do the work of an evangelist, make full proof of thy ministry." Paul's charge includes *clear thinking*:

"But watch thou in all things." It includes *patient suffering*: "Endure afflictions." It includes *intentional witnessing*: "Do the work of an evangelist." It includes *faithful laboring*: "Make full proof of thy ministry." Above all else, Christ has called us to be faithful. This alone must be the principle from which our ministry flows and the objective at which our ministry aims. We must look to the day when we will hear our Master say, "Well done, thou good and faithful servant" (Matt. 25:21).

Bibliography

Azurdia, Art. "Recovering the Third Mark of the Church." *Reformation and Revival* 3 (1994): 61–79.

Baxter, Richard. *The Practical Works of Richard Baxter: Select Treatises.* Reprint, Grand Rapids: Baker, 1981.

Boice, James M. *Romans: The New Humanity.* Grand Rapids: Baker, 1995.

Bolton, Robert. *The Carnal Professor, Discovering the Woeful Slavery of a Man Guided by the Flesh.* Reprint, Ligonier, Pa.: Soli Deo Gloria, 1992.

Bunyan, John. *The Holy War: The Losing and Taking Again of the Town of Mansoul.* Grand Rapids: Baker, 1991.

———. *The Pilgrim's Progress.* Uhrichsville, Ohio: Barbour, 1985.

Calvin, John. *Institutes of the Christian Religion.* Edited by J. T. McNeill. Translated by Ford Lewis Battles. Philadelphia, Pa.: Westminster, 1960.

Carson, Don. *A Call to Spiritual Reformation: Priorities from Paul and His Prayers.* Grand Rapids: Baker, 1992.

———. *The Sermon on the Mount: An Evangelical Exposition of Matthew 5–7.* Grand Rapids: Baker, 1978.

Edwards, Jonathan. *Charity and Its Fruits: Christian Love as Manifested in the Heart and Life.* Edinburgh: Banner of Truth, 2000.

———. *Religious Affections.* Minneapolis: Bethany House, 1996.

Flavel, John. *The Works of John Flavel.* Reprint, London: Banner of Truth, 1968.

Gouge, William. *Of Domesticall Duties: Eight Treatises.* London, 1622.

Hendriksen, William. *The New Testament Commentary: Exposition of Ephesians.* Grand Rapids: Baker, 1987.

Lloyd-Jones, Martyn. *Studies in the Sermon on the Mount: Volumes 1–2.* Grand Rapids: Eerdmans, 1962.

———. *The Unsearchable Riches of Christ: An Exposition of Ephesians 3.* Grand Rapids: Baker, 2003.

Lunde, Jonathan. *Following Jesus, the Servant King: A Biblical Theology of Covenantal Discipleship.* Grand Rapids: Zondervan, 2010.

Mohler, Albert. "Church Discipline: The Missing Mark." *The Southern Baptist Journal of Theology* 4 (2000): 16.

Owen, John. *The Works of John Owen.* Edited by W. H. Gould. Reprint, Edinburgh: Banner of Truth, 1977.

Pearse, Edward. *The Best Match; or, The Soul's Espousal to Christ.* Morgan, Pa.: Soli Deo Gloria, 1994.

Perkins, William. *A Godly and Learned Exposition upon Christ's Sermon on the Mount.* Vol. 3, *The Works of William Perkins.* London: John Legate, 1631.

Pink, A. W. *Gleanings from Paul: Studies in the Prayers of the Apostle.* Edinburgh: Banner of Truth, 2006.

Piper, John. *Brothers, We Are Not Professionals: A Plea to Pastors for Radical Ministry.* Nashville: Broadman & Holman, 2002.

Stevenson, Robert L. *Robert Louis Stevenson: Four Complete Novels.* New York: Gramercy, 1995.

Stott, John. *The Living Church.* Downers Grove, Ill.: InterVarsity, 2007.

Strauch, Alexander. *Leading with Love.* Littleton, Colo.: Lewis and Roth, 2006.

Swinnock, George. *The Works of George Swinnock.* 5 vols. Reprint, Edinburgh: Banner of Truth, 1992.

Thomas, I. D. E., ed. *A Puritan Golden Treasury.* Edinburgh: Banner of Truth, 2000.

Tozer, A. W. *The Pursuit of God.* Radford, Va.: Wilder, 2008.

Tripp, Paul. *Dangerous Calling: Confronting the Unique Challenges of Pastoral Ministry.* Wheaton, Ill.: Crossway, 2012.

Warfield, B. B. "The Authority and Inspiration of the Scriptures." *Westminster Teacher* (September 1889), n.p. Available online at http://www.theologynetwork.org/christian-beliefs/the-bible/the-authority-and-inspiration-of-the-scriptures.htm.

Wells, David F. *No Place for Truth; or, Whatever Happened to Evangelical Theology?* Grand Rapids: Eerdmans, 1993.

Whyte, Alexander. *Bible Characters: The New Testament.* London: Oliphants, 1952.